CONCEPTIONS OF LITERACY

CONCEPTIONS OF LITERACY

Graduate Instructors and the
Teaching of First-Year Composition

MEAGHAN BREWER

UTAH STATE UNIVERSITY PRESS
Logan

Published by Utah State University Press
An imprint of University Press of Colorado
245 Century Circle, Suite 202
Louisville, Colorado 80027

ASSOCIATION
of UNIVERSITY
PRESSES

The University Press of Colorado is a proud member of
the Association of University Presses.

The University Press of Colorado is a cooperative publishing enterprise sup-
ported, in part, by Adams State University, Colorado State University, Fort
Lewis College, Metropolitan State University of Denver, Regis University,
University of Colorado, University of Northern Colorado, University of
Wyoming, Utah State University, and Western Colorado University.

∞ This paper meets the requirements of the ANSI/NISO Z39.48–1992
(Permanence of Paper)

ISBN: 978-1-60732-933-6 (paperback)
ISBN: 978-1-60732-934-3 (ebook)
https://doi.org/10.7330/9781607329343

Library of Congress Cataloging-in-Publication Data

Names: Brewer, Meaghan, author.
Title: Conceptions of literacy : graduate instructors and the teaching of first-
    year composition / Meaghan Brewer.
Description: Logan : Utah State University Press, an imprint of University Press
    of Colorado, [2019]. | Includes bibliographical references and index.
Identifiers: LCCN 2019034586 (print) | LCCN 2019034587 (ebook) | ISBN
    9781607329336 (paperback) | ISBN 9781607329343 (ebook)
Subjects: LCSH: Composition (Language arts)—Study and teaching.
Classification: LCC LB1575.8 .B73 2019 (print) | LCC LB1575.8 (ebook) | DDC
    372.6—dc23
LC record available at https://lccn.loc.gov/2019034586
LC ebook record available at https://lccn.loc.gov/2019034587

Modified portions of chapter 3 appeared in "'The Text Is the Thing': Graduate
Students in Literature and Cultural Conceptions of Literacy," *Composition
Forum* 42 (Fall 2019).

The University Press of Colorado gratefully acknowledges the generous support of Pace University toward the publication of this book.

For Jon, Jillian, and Jeremy

CONTENTS

PREFACE

The Fall Practicum at Public University

It's the first day of the fall Graduate Teaching Practicum at Public University, and the classroom, a tiny seminar room tucked away in the corner of an office module on the eleventh floor, is HOT. I come into an already crowded room and have to squeeze behind the chair of one of the male graduate students to get in. I realize I don't remember any of the practicum students' names from when I met them last week during orientation, a potential challenge given that I'm going to be taking field notes on what they say today.

I start to take out my laptop, and Lily, who I later learn is a first-year student in the PhD program who plans to specialize in composition and rhetoric, starts talking to me about her first day. "After this first week, I started to get nervous about the fact that I signed up for the study. Someone's going to have to observe this disaster!" When I ask her what happened, it's not a big deal. One student looked at the clock and Lily thought, "Oh my gosh, am I boring him?" But then she realized she used to look at the clock a lot in class too, and she was a good student.

The other issue was that her classroom was stifling. "I mean, my classroom was really, really hot, and I was sweating!" she told me. I reassure her that the same thing had happened to me and that her students were probably sweating too. "Yeah, but I was nervous, and being nervous makes you sweat more," she said. I think to myself that Lily probably had a successful first week—the fact that these were the problems says a lot about how smoothly everything else must have run. But Lily, along

DOI: 10.7330/9781607329343.c000

with many of the other graduate students, is concerned with things other than the theory behind teaching composition. Physiological things! And their concerns aren't so different from the concerns I seem to experience anew every semester.

David, the practicum instructor, gets the class started by unrolling long sheaves of drawing paper onto the tables we're crowded around and asking everyone to draw a representation of their classroom during the first week. The graduate students start sketching out desks arranged into circles (in their orientation the previous week, they were told to use this arrangement in their classes). As Lily's comments forecast, a number of them draw images of themselves with sweat or heat waves emanating from them. After drawing, everyone switches with a partner and then interprets their picture. David then asks about common threads in the pictures.

As I sit in on this classroom scene, participating in the drawing but also careful to take notes I can refer to later, I experience a moment of what Sigmund Freud ([1919] 2003) called the "uncanny," wherein something familiar is made strange. Freud describes wandering through a small town in Italy and finding himself accidentally circling back to the same area. I too had been here before, in this very classroom, four years earlier, in another practicum course taught by David. Although this practicum is different, if only because of the different people in the room, it is also uncannily the same, especially at moments when David repeats an idea I remember him talking about before or engages us in a similar activity. For a fleeting moment, I feel as if my past and present selves are juxtaposed onto each other, and I wonder how *I* changed during the semester I took the practicum and how those changes have continued over the years that followed.

I am here because of questions about how ways of valuing literacy shape pedagogy for new teachers. These questions first came to me when I was working with preservice education students in a writing center for middle-grades students I set up in an elementary school a few blocks from Public U's campus. Each group of preservice-education students worked in a cohort with two or three other preservice educators to develop lesson plans for their middle schoolers. Because they saw their students so infrequently (just once a week), I emphasized that they needed to create lesson sequences to encourage transfer of ideas between sessions. However, I was often surprised at the choices these preservice educators were making about what to teach. As soon as I began asking them how they decided to teach what they were teaching, I recognized that the pedagogical choices they were making reflected different ways of valuing literacy and that my hesitance about some of these choices reflected differences between how I conceptualized literacy and how they did.

One of the preservice instructors I worked with, an older student I'll call Connie, who had worked in instructional technology in a library at a high school for ten years, opened her lesson by writing on the easel we were using as a chalkboard, "Today we are all writers." She passed around a sheet of stickers to the students with smiley faces and phrases like "Awesome Job" and "You're special!" When I asked her about this later on, she recalled a student at the high school where she worked asking her, "Why don't teachers give out stickers anymore?" Connie told me, "We all like to be rewarded. We all like to know we're doing a good job." Connie's lesson was on choosing a personal event for narrative writing, but the strategy she was teaching seemed almost secondary to the purpose of building students' esteem. "Kid spelling is okay today!" she wrote on the easel.

I was initially skeptical about Connie's decision to pass around stickers with such clichéd and, I thought, infantile reminders of each student's inherent self-worth, thinking this group, mostly seventh graders, would dismiss her lesson as silly or babyish. My objection had to do with the fact that making the students feel good about themselves seemed, at several points, to take precedence over what I considered the more important goal of improving their ability to talk about texts and ideas critically. I was surprised, however, when the students really got into what she was saying and began the writing activity she constructed, which involved brainstorming to find a personal event to write a narrative about, with an enthusiasm I had not seen from them during previous sessions. Connie told me later, "Personal narrative lets you get to know your students. It's so important to get to know your students on a personal level." For Connie, personal reasons for writing took precedence.

After I talked this lesson over with Connie, I found out that her reason for constructing the lesson so closely around personal motivations for writing was that she herself was feeling insecure about her return to school after so long. She worried in particular about a Victorian poetry class in which her professor had asked her to rewrite a paper on Tennyson three times. Connie's professor had told her she had to stop writing about her feelings and instead focus on taking apart the text—essentially, Connie heard from him that what she felt, the effect the text had on her, didn't matter. Consequently, in her lesson she was giving her students the very thing she felt had been taken from her.

Observing and giving feedback to Connie and her peers involved my recognizing not just where these conceptualizations of literacy came from but also how my own conception of literacy shaped how I prioritized certain lessons and encounters with literacy in my teaching. Whereas I saw literacy in largely social, communal ways, as the means with which people create relationships with others, Connie saw it in mostly individual terms. And these conceptions of literacy were influenced by past (and present) experiences and literacy sponsors.

These questions continued once I began to lead teaching circles for first-year writing courses in which we evaluated student papers and portfolios together. During one teaching circle, another composition instructor proclaimed she would give a D to one of my student's papers, which I had brought in as an example of a B-range paper. As we discussed the reasons for such disparate views of the same paper, I realized her evaluation stemmed from some punctuation errors, a few comma splices and misused semicolons, and the student's use of past tense in reference to texts, all of which I had deemed relatively minor. This instructor gave more precedence to what I would label as *mistakes that don't interfere with meaning* than I had in my evaluation. Encountering a vision of literacy different from my own forced me not only to think about where these views came from but also to reevaluate my own views on literacy, to recognize them as ideological.

As this last statement reflects, this book is also a personal journey for me into examining where my own understandings of literacy come from and how I have channeled them into my teaching and scholarly practice. As one of the participants in Elizabeth Rankin's (1994) study of new graduate instructors said to her, "This is your story. . . . This is really about you" (42). Many of my realizations about the ways my own literacy background and experiences have shaped me occurred in parallel with discussions with the graduate instructors who took part in this study and in my analysis of their data. In the process of examining the literacy conceptions of the seven focal participants in my study, I was also continually reflecting on my own literacy conception and how it had changed since I was enrolled in the same practicum course. As the daughter of a British Romanticist, I probably had traces of the cultural-literacy conception I will discuss in chapter 4. My mother, who worked as a school media specialist and later in a public library, emphasized what I call *literacy for personal growth* in her focus on reading for enjoyment. Books and academia played an influential role in my development. As a child, I was often tailing behind my father on campus with my three younger siblings or wandering the rows of books at the university library. The implicit messages about literacy I learned in my childhood formed conceptions of literacy I had to think about more critically when I entered graduate school with the intention of pursuing a career in composition. As it was for many of these graduate instructors, the field of rhetoric and composition was largely alien to me when I began my program, and this unfamiliarity presented challenges as I embarked on my first semester of teaching. Thus, while I endeavor to represent the graduate instructors in the study informing this book as fully as possible, I recognize that, as Rankin (1994) claims, "All ethnographers are colonizers" (42).

To put it another way, I am always viewing the graduate instructors' conceptions of literacy through the lens of my own conception and in ways that can't be fully unraveled from their stories.

An example of the way my own lenses may have impacted the way I collected and interpreted the data presented in this book is that I recognize now I felt much more at ease with the women participants than with the men. As I look through the interview data, I see I was more apt to push the women to articulate the reasoning behind some of their philosophies and teaching practices than I was the men, and I also felt better able to interpret their interview data. To put it another way, I felt I "knew" them better, a feeling that continues today, as I'm still in touch with all the women who participated in my study but none of the men. I identified the most with Jordi, a graduate instructor who, like me, had an English-professor father. Jordi and I both initially resisted following our fathers' career trajectories; while I channeled my resistance into pursuing a PhD in rhetoric and composition (instead of literature), Jordi chose to study American instead of British literature.

Perhaps because of this identification, a colleague who read an early draft of this book commented that I invested the most disappointment in Jordi as a participant, especially in the moments when her ideological positions seemed to match mine the least. While I have since revised in order to offer (I hope) more compassionate readings of all the graduate instructors who participated in the study informing this book, I note my identification with Jordi to point to the very human element of research, as well as of WPA work. As WPAs and pedagogy instructors, we *feel* graduate students are being unfair when they bash a theorist we like or when they seem to just "not get it," and these feelings can affect our ability to engage new graduate instructors' preconceptions and see where these preconceptions are coming from.

To account, if only partially, for the inherent situatedness of my role as I researcher, I include detailed quotes from the graduate instructors' interviews and literacy narratives throughout this book as a way of foregrounding their voices. Although I act as interpreter here, the inclusion of these quotes also enables readers to make up their own minds about what these data indicate, perhaps considering them in light of their own studies and experiences of how we educate new graduate instructors. Indeed, since what I offer here, in considering the idea of conceptions of literacy, is an interpretive framework for understanding the ideological positions of new graduate instructors, I hope what follows has practical use for not only instructors of practicum courses but also for graduate instructors in identifying and reflecting on their positions and how their past experiences with teaching and literacy have informed them. The goal is for readers to recognize themselves and their students in the case studies of new graduate instructors I present. For new graduate instructors, this study might provide the opportunity for them to identify preexisting views they are only tacitly aware they hold. For practica instructors and writing program administrators, I hope it reminds us to be patient with new graduate instructors rather than dismissing or feeling frustrated with them. New graduate instructors are faced with an almost impossible task of, as one my participants pointed out, both being and becoming, often with relatively little support, someone they not only haven't been before but haven't seen before. Yet, as with our undergraduates, they also come to our practica with "funds of knowledge" we can help them mobilize *if* we (and they) understand more fully their ideological positions (Moll et al. 1992).

ACKNOWLEDGMENTS

Writing a book, I now know, is a tremendous undertaking. Although I spent countless hours working on this book alone at my computer, I could not have done so were it not for an extensive network of support that began years ago as the ideas for this book were first germinating.

My first thank you goes to my editor at Utah State University Press, Michael Spooner, who believed in this book before it was a book and shepherded me through my first round of peer reviews. Rachael Levay took over the project without skipping a beat when Michael retired and has taught me much about the publishing process. Both Michael and Rachael were responsive, supportive, and wise, and I could not have done this without them. I must also extend a heartfelt thank you to the anonymous reviewers of this book for their pointed, detailed, and wise comments. I know the kind of work and time both must have spent with this manuscript, and it is truly better for their guidance.

I was incredibly lucky to have worked with such supportive and intelligent colleagues throughout this process. The idea for the study informing this book began to take form in a coffee shop during a meeting with Michael W. Smith and Eli Goldblatt. Many of my "aha!" moments occurred as I puzzled through data in their offices, over the phone, and at academic conferences. Their thoughtful wisdom will be with me in every class I teach and every piece of scholarly work I undertake. Steve Newman brought a literary studies perspective and helped me think through the historical origins of the conceptions of literacy I describe. Jessica Restaino introduced me to the body of work on graduate instructors, teaching, and graduate practica in composition and has given me the tough but crucial feedback every writer needs. Lori Salem and Rebekah Buchanan helped me with an early study on how preservice educators decide what to teach, which ended up serving as an inspiration for this project. Christine Farris offered sage advice on one of my chapters during the Research Network Workshop at the Rhetoric Society of America conference.

As I revised my early manuscript into a book, I had to make difficult decisions about what to cut out of a huge 460-page manuscript, as well as how to shape it into something that responded more pointedly to important questions in the field. I could not have done so without the support of my colleagues at Pace University, including Erica Johnson, Sid Ray, Helane Levine-Keating, Mark Hussey, Sarah Blackwood, Stephanie Hsu, Steve Goldleaf, Eugene Richie, Ebele Oseye, Martha Driver, Catherine Zimmer, Rita Bradshaw-Beyers, Charles North, Agie Markiewicz-Hocking, Tran Tran, and Kelley Kreitz. Brice Particelli, Kung-wan Philip Choong, Mara Grayson, and Laurie McMillan all served as writing buddies and read and responded to chapter drafts, many of which were far, far too long. Finally, Kristen di Gennaro, through her thoughtful responses to my drafts and long conversations that took place in our offices or on New Jersey transit trains, acted as a mentor and crucial sounding board as I tested out new ideas, pushed my arguments, and asked the difficult questions that would shape the final version of this book.

My husband, Jonathan Wert, helped me draft my research protocol for the study informing this book for the Institutional Review Board and has been a constant source of encouragement. Jon, I will always remember and appreciate the countless hours you did your own thing or (later) took care of our daughter while I answered the siren call of my computer. My daughter Jillian learned early in her young life that sometimes Mommy just needs to write and was often waiting with a hug and a new drawing as soon as I logged off my computer. My mother-in-law and father-in-law, Sylvia and Mike Wert, took her to the library and to lunch and otherwise entertained her when I needed extra time to work. I also want to thank my parents, William and Tracy Brewer, and my siblings, Kirsten, Rori, and Aidan, for encouraging me to pursue a career in composition and rhetoric in the first place. Part of my desire to explore the literacy conceptions of the participants in this study is motivated by my position as the daughter of an English professor and a library media specialist. I am grateful to my parents for always believing in me and for buying me books, even when it seemed like I already owned every book on Greek mythology ever written.

I would also like to thank the graduate instructors who participated in the study informing this book. Barbara, Blake, Garrett, Jordi, Karen, Lily, and Max all opened up to me in ways I never could have imagined and gave me the great gift of their time during their busy first year of teaching. They were patient with my questions and thoughtful in their responses, and it is to them I owe thanks for the richness of the data that inform this book.

CONCEPTIONS OF LITERACY

1

INTRODUCTION
A Framework for Understanding the
Experiences of New Graduate Instructors

*The blank page awaits the writer's first sentence, while new
teachers, charged with the task of getting students to write
and navigating new graduate programs themselves, are largely
untrained, unsure of their responsibilities, and equipped with
a syllabus that they did not design and perhaps a list of pedagogical procedures they do not understand.*

—Jessica Restaino

The above epigraph points to a central tension in the field of
composition: although scholars have worked hard to theorize
the teaching of writing and develop best practices for educating
composition instructors, most of the work of teaching writing
is done by graduate students and adjuncts with very little formal education in pedagogy, many of whom would not identify
as readers or writers of composition theory. Understanding the
needs and attitudes of new graduate instructors is especially important given that they teach almost a quarter of composition
classes, according to a study done by Anne Ruggles Gere (2009)
of 643 writing programs in the 2008–2009 academic year (4).
Extrapolating from these numbers, Dylan Dryer (2012) points
out that graduate instructors taught "nearly a *quarter-million* undergraduates" in the institutions Gere surveyed alone (446n2).[1]
Yet, as a field grappling with historical and institutional realities
that are often not conducive to giving these new teachers the resources they need, gaps still remain in our understanding of the
experiences of new graduate instructors, and there are very few

DOI: 10.7330/9781607329343.c001

recent, in-depth empirically based guides for teacher education in composition.

Perhaps not surprisingly, studies on graduate-teacher education often address issues of identity, and, in particular, how graduate instructors[2] negotiate prior identities while being asked to take on a new identity as a teacher of writing. That is, implicit in these studies is the assumption that new graduate instructors arrive to their first semester of teaching already having a number of experiences with literacy and education that shape their conceptions of what kinds of teachers they should be. In their study of graduate instructors at George Mason and Boise State, E. Shelley Reid, Heidi Estrem, and Marcia Belcheir (2012) found that "TAs were influenced more strongly by prior personal experiences and beliefs . . . than by their formal pedagogy education" (33–34). Dryer (2012) argues that new graduate instructors "bring their cultural history" to their teaching and coursework (422). Barbara Cole and Arabella Lyon (2008) also found that graduate students come to their first semester of teaching with "well-established" but often "problematic ideologies" that affect their "*writerly*" and "*teacherly self*" (Cole and Lyon 2008, 194–95).

Despite this recurrent finding, very few studies on graduate-instructor education have attempted to define and operationalize this "identity," "prior personal experiences and beliefs," or "cultural history," even as they identify the influence these constructs have on their teaching. In other words, more studies are needed that define what we mean by these terms, break them down into key, measurable concepts, and then test these concepts by applying them to data collected from participants in graduate-teacher-education programs. The goal of this book is to fill this void.

This book uses the lens of new literacy studies, and work on defining and categorizing different views of literacy, to argue that graduate instructors' attitudes toward and beliefs about language and literacy (which are realized through and overlap with their identities) are an important source they draw on as they conceptualize what it means to teach composition in their first year. Graduate instructors' literacy beliefs have long existed as a faint thread throughout the research on composition teacher education. By this I mean scholars have noted these attitudes in passing or perhaps to characterize a particular graduate instructor participating in a study but have not made them the focus of their research. Rankin (1994), for example, describes graduate instructors who want to teach personal writing and help students claim an authentic "voice" (30–31). Wendy Bishop (1990) and Jessica Restaino (2012) both describe participants who view writing largely as grammar or a set of neutral skills. Much of this research attests to the importance of these conceptions in terms of how they translate to new graduate instructors' teaching. Reid, Estrem, and Belcheir (2012), for example, describe how their participants' teaching "principles" come from their identities as poets and writers (47). However, none of these studies have made graduate instructors' conceptions of literacy the focal point of research.

By using a literacy studies framework, I hope to offer a fuller picture of the sets of values and beliefs new graduate instructors have when they enter our pedagogy courses or other teacher-education programs. Often, past experiences with literacy are not the main focus (Bishop 1990; Rankin 1994), or (as in Reid, Estrem, and Belcheir [2012] above) research examines graduate instructors' attitudes only towards *writing*, and specifically academic writing, without discussing other aspects of literacy that might inform how they feel about their own writing or their students' (see also Dryer 2012; Ebest 2005; Farris 1996; Reid 2009). While this research has been illuminating, it has stopped short of capturing how literacy experiences and sponsors beyond academic writing have shaped new graduate instructors. For example, one of the graduate instructors whose story I tell had lived in a yoga ashram, an experience that deeply shaped her understanding of literacy and writing pedagogy. Another was influenced by being homeschooled in a conservative Protestant home. Although many of the graduate instructors' encounters with academic writing had also shaped them, the term *literacy* (and an orientation towards the insights of new literacy studies) more fully captures their participation in the various cultures that would come to define how they viewed themselves as teachers of writing. Moreover, focusing on new graduate instructors' literacy conceptions allows those in mentoring relationships with new graduate instructors to more adequately account for and perhaps even anticipate some of the struggles they will have in coming to terms with the composition pedagogy explicitly and implicitly advocated for in graduate practica and standardized curricula for first-year composition (FYC).

In what follows, I describe an empirical study that examines the conceptions of literacy of seven graduate instructors, four women and three men, enrolled in graduate programs in English literature, rhetoric and composition, and creative writing who were teaching their first semester of composition at a large, public university in an urban area in the Northeast. I then turn to a theoretical framework for understanding these graduate instructors' attitudes and beliefs about literacy I call *conceptions of literacy* and give overviews of seven different conceptions that comprise this framework: literacy for personal growth, literacy for social growth, social/critical literacy, critical activism literacy, cultural literacy, functionalist literacy, and instrumental literacy. Finally, I situate this study and framework in the literature on graduate-instructor education and mentoring, focusing specifically on the two themes that appear most regularly in this research: identity and resistance.

Although past studies (Dobrin 2005; Ebest 2005; Welch 1993) have pointed to the ideological and identity-changing nature of the practicum course, in this book I argue, along with recent studies by Dryer (2012) and Reid, Estrem, and Belcheir (2012), that the practicum course has limited and uneven *visible* effects on graduate instructors' identities and pedagogy. I say *visible* because my interpretation of the data does show that the practicum has an effect but that it may not be easy to see for practica instructors or even the graduate instructors themselves. The graduate instructors in this study came to their first semester of teaching composition with ingrained literacy worldviews, and these sets of attitudes and beliefs appeared to guide them in their pedagogical decisions more than did their formal pedagogy education. For example, Lily, the PhD student in rhetoric and composition I mention earlier, wanted her students to be "authentic" and "soulful" in what they thought, did, and said (pers. comm., October 15, 2010). On the other hand, Barbara, a second-year fiction MFA student, was influenced by her participation in online feminist communities to see literacy in more social, communal ways and to look for strategies to empower students by engaging their critical literacy. Often, the graduate instructors were only tacitly aware of how invested they were in these belief systems and the extent to which these systems were predetermining their decisions about how to teach composition.

As these statements suggest, these conceptions influenced how they encountered the concepts from composition studies presented in the practicum course and enacted them in the classroom. Whereas Barbara's teaching seemed most in line with the ideas communicated in the graduate practicum, Lily often diverged from the master syllabus the graduate instructors were supposed to follow in order to match her prior assumption that engaging her students in their writing had to happen alongside a process of self-actualization. What I would like to suggest, and explore further in this book, is not the contention that any one conception of literacy is right or wrong but rather that practica instructors and writing program administrators must be aware of graduate instructors' conceptions of literacy in order to better support them in the long, developmental process of becoming teachers. Because conceptions of literacy are learned over time, and because they are worldviews deeply entwined with and enacted through identity, understanding new graduate instructors' conceptions of literacy offers a way of seeing them in terms not of deficit but rather of the understandings they bring with them to teaching writing.

THE SETTING: PUBLIC UNIVERSITY AND
THE GRADUATE PRACTICUM

Public University is a large, research-intensive public university in an urban area near the East Coast. The English department at Public University has over thirty tenured or tenure-track faculty, thirty-five non-tenure-track faculty, and over sixty adjunct faculty. Of the tenured and tenure-track faculty, around six teach graduate creative writing courses and identify as creative writers and only three teach and identify as scholars in rhetoric and composition. The composition faculty and the first-year writing program (FYWP) are both part of the English department, which could be considered "traditional" in that it maintains a heavy literature emphasis. This emphasis is important in the context of this study because it reinforces the sense of the practicum as a contested space, existing within but also on the outskirts of graduate students' curricular requirements.

The graduate instructors were required to participate in a week-long workshop led by the practicum instructor, David, immediately prior to the start of the semester and then enroll in the practicum course concurrently with their first semester of teaching.[3] The FYWP also provided a system of support and mentoring beyond the practicum. Graduate instructors in their first semester of teaching met weekly in small groups with one of two graduate mentors for more informal support. After this first semester, the FYWP required instructors to participate in teaching circles led by experienced instructors that met three times during the semester, with the final meeting acting as a norming and grading session.

Despite this continued mentoring, for many graduate students outside composition, the practicum would be the only exposure they would have to composition theory. Again, research on mentoring and educating graduate instructors suggests this is not particular to Public. As Albert Kitzhaber argues, the graduate practicum has historically been viewed as existing in the shadows of "'the headier regions of the teaching of literature'" (quoted in Dobrin 2005, 11). Sidney Dobrin (2005) attests that this course has always been a subject of contention, citing scholars who have argued it should either not have any place in the graduate curriculum at all or exist only tangentially. As a result, as Ebest (2005) argues, for many graduate students, "composition studies remains a boring, blurry sub-discipline"

(5). The graduate instructors in the current study confirmed that they often heard from English department faculty (outside composition) that their role as graduate students was to become scholars, not teachers, and that they should not invest extra time in learning composition pedagogy. This programmatic lack of emphasis on the practicum (even though it is a credit-bearing, graded course) and other aspects of graduate instructors' teaching by professors outside the FYWP is unfortunate, given its importance in providing an early foundation for their teaching (see Miller et al. 2005).

As at many other universities, the practicum and the FYWP had what I would describe as a strong social/critical emphasis. At its inception, the FYWP based its curriculum on David Bartholomae's (1985) conception in "Inventing the University" of writing as socially constructed within discourse communities and of the university as comprising several discourse communities, which students must learn to appropriate. To accomplish these goals, the course description in the handbook designed for FYW instructors emphasizes cross curricular approaches to teaching writing, critical reading and writing, and instruction in rhetorical strategies. Although experienced instructors in the FYWP were invited to design their own syllabi, the program also created a "common" or standard syllabus for its first-year courses, which included four total courses, including two levels of composition, as well as ESL sections of each of these two courses. Most students entering Public University as undergraduates place into the second, non-ESL course, which the graduate instructors in the practicum taught and which I refer to as College Composition (CC).

The common syllabus for CC, which the graduate instructors in the practicum were required to use, was designed to have first-year students explore ideas such as nonviolent protest through the teachings of Gandhi and his followers; the legacy of westward expansion and historical rhetoric surrounding the American "frontier;" and slavery through the lens of science fiction. The text adopted by the FYWP was Bedford/St. Martin's *Cultural Conversations: The Presence of the Past*, a themed reader whose readings were meant to encourage students to adopt a critical view of present cultural ideas by viewing them through the lens of the past (Dilks, Hansen, and Parfitt 2001). The final text for the class was Octavia Butler's *Kindred* (2003), a science-fiction novel in which two individuals from the 1970s, an African American woman and her Caucasian husband, travel back in time to a plantation in the antebellum South.

Like the course Dobrin (2005) describes, the practicum at Public University sought not so much to encourage graduate instructors to think "about how to teach, but about how they think of themselves as teachers and as writers" (20). By this, I mean that whereas the practicum exposed the graduate instructors to composition theory and pedagogy and modeled practical pedagogical strategies (like using small groups, having students arrange desks in a circle, and meeting with students one on one to guide them in revision), graduate instructors weren't pushed to assume any particular identity as an instructor or even necessarily to adopt a particular composition pedagogy. David facilitated graduate instructors' coming to their own teaching identities throughout the semester, in particular through in-class journal entries, such as one during orientation week that asked the graduate instructors to "write about an influential teacher" (field notes, August 25, 2010). Perhaps the most significant contemplation of themselves as teachers occurred in the autobiographical literacy narratives the graduate instructors wrote as an assignment for the practicum course, one shorter one that they turned in early in the semester and a longer, revised narrative they turned in as part of their final teaching portfolio, which they revised to reflect what they learned about themselves during the semester. David met with each of the graduate instructors to ask them questions about the first literacy narrative and to prompt them to think critically about the experiences they described.

The fact that the literacy narratives composed a large part of the writing for the practicum sent a message to the graduate instructors that the experiences they brought to this first semester of teaching were significant and that, moreover, reflecting on these experiences would be essential to their growth as teachers and scholars. David was very different from the dogmatic, inflexible mentors described by Nancy Welch (1993), who repeatedly and contemptuously called her beliefs about writing and the world into question, promoting a "conversion" model of graduate-teacher education. Rather, David encouraged each graduate instructor to come to their understanding of literacy and pedagogy in their own way.

However, as Bishop (1990) states, "No teacher training program or pedagogy seminar can . . . be ideologically neutral" (xv). At some points, David expressed frustration when graduate instructors misinterpreted ideas presented by the practicum readings, displaying some of the "anxieties" Reid (2007) describes as an understandable by-product of the fact that graduate instructors are often not ready to learn ideas just because practica instructors are ready to teach them. This disconnect was especially the case during the two classes in which the graduate instructors discussed articles they had read by Bartholomae and Susan Jarratt. After both classes, David theorized that the graduate instructors simply did not have enough disciplinary knowledge of rhetoric and composition to interpret these readings. That is, like Douglas Hesse (1993), he traced their "resistance" to their inexperience with the terms, history, and values characterizing the discourse community of composition (227).

David also postulated that the graduate instructors thought Bartholomae's "Inventing the University" was beneath them—that because it was about students learning to write, it should be easier and more straightforward than, say, an article about literary theory. David's comments after these classes say a great deal about how much our (WPAs' and pedagogy instructors') anxieties about graduate instructor "resistance" are wrapped up in anxieties about our discipline and how it is perceived by outsiders. WPAs and other composition scholars have long had to defend the importance and scholarly nature of our work to outsiders, including members of our universities and even colleagues in our own departments. As Jennifer Grouling (2015) contends, "The inclusion of composition theory [in the practicum] has to do with sharing our disciplinary expertise and being taken seriously." Moreover, as other scholars have argued, the practicum course is a crucial site wherein new graduate instructors acquire disciplinary knowledge that can inform and help them reflect on their teaching practice (Ryan and Graban 2009; Stancliff and Goggin 2007).

However, Grouling (2015) also points out that our desire to get students to see composition as a not just a set of courses but as an intellectual field with its own content can also work against us, suggesting that some graduate instructors, in connecting to composition theory only "as graduate students," make the common graduate-seminar move of looking for ways to challenge it without the balancing move of also considering what it would look like to enact these principles in their classrooms. WPAs may feel especially hurt by this "resistance" because they see composition theory as part of their own identities. David got past his frustration by realizing that what appeared to be resistance could more accurately be described as moments when graduate instructors were confronting their own tacit beliefs about literacy, moments that put their literacy ideologies and the ones being presented in the practicum on a "collision course" (to use Russel Durst's [1999] terminology). That is, their "resistance" was not simply stubbornness, nor was it necessarily counterproductive. Rather, it signaled the understandable fear of having one's worldview challenged and could even (as in the case of a graduate instructor I describe in the next chapter) act as a precursor to learning.

THE STUDY AND PARTICIPANTS

I recruited participants from the fall 2010 graduate practicum. Of the eighteen practicum students, ten were enrolled in the master of fine arts program in creative writing, six were in the PhD program in English with a concentration in literature, and two were in the PhD in English program with a concentration in rhetoric and composition. The fact that only two out of eighteen students identified with the field of rhetoric and composition impacted the culture of the practicum. Although all the students were engaged in the subject matter of the course and many looked to David, the practicum instructor, for guidance beyond teaching in their first semester, the preponderance of graduate instructors did not identify the subject matter of the practicum as their primary field of study.

Sixteen of the eighteen graduate instructors volunteered to participate. Although I gathered data from all these participants to give me a broad sense of trends in their beliefs about literacy, I chose seven graduate instructors to focus most of my analysis on. I selected these graduate instructors with an eye to having participants representing all three disciplines (comp/rhet, literature, and creative writing) and to including different genders from each discipline.[4] Because I was teaching on two campuses during the semesters I collected data, I also selected participants whose classes were scheduled at times I could observe them. All these focal participants identified as Caucasian. While I recognize this as an unfortunate limitation of the study, the participants represented the overall demographic of the class.[5]

The following table lists the participants and some of their demographic information. Under "Teaching experience," I indicate whether the graduate instructors had any previous teaching experiences, even if it was tutoring or working as a teaching assistant, as is the case for Garrett and Jordi, who worked as assistants for large literature survey classes in their first two years in their programs. "Solo" indicates that the graduate instructor had experience planning lessons and managing their own classroom without the presence of a supervisor or other instructor.

My goal for the study was to collect data that would give me a detailed depiction not only of the conception of literacy each participant held but also of some possible influences for this conception. In order to triangulate graduate instructors' attitudes towards literacy across different data types, I conducted three interviews with each participant, including an initial interview in the fall semester and two interviews (one in the fall and another the following spring) after observing their classes. I also

Table 1.1. Brief descriptions of the seven focal participants

Graduate instructor	Program of study	Age at time of study	Teaching experience	Year in program
Lily	composition and rhetoric	26	solo, tutoring (adults)	1
Karen	composition and rhetoric	41	solo (secondary school)	1
Barbara	creative writing	27	tutoring (primary school)	2
Max	creative writing	22	no	1
Garrett	literature	27	literature TA	3
Blake	literature	23	tutoring (primary school)	1
Jordi	literature	27	literature TA	3

collected both their initial and revised literacy narratives and took field notes from my visits to the classes they were teaching and from the practicum. (For a more detailed list of these data-collection instruments, see appendix A.) In the following chapters, I use details from these graduate instructors' literacy narratives and interview data to tell their stories in more depth.

CONCEPTIONS OF LITERACY: DEFINITIONS AND THEORETICAL BACKGROUND

Although the term *literacy* is ubiquitous in literature on teacher education in composition, to date, no studies have attempted to understand new graduate instructors' experiences through the lens of literacy theory, and none have attempted to understand these experiences specifically by exploring graduate instructors' literacy worldviews. This gap in the research is perhaps because the concept of literacy is inherently varied and slippery. Many today, even in professional educational organizations, describe literacy either as reading and writing or as knowledge of a particular area or field, as in math literacy or information literacy. However, these ways of seeing literacy fail to recognize the socially situated, multimodal, and multifaceted nature of literacy practices. Sylvia Scribner (1984) argues that no universal definition of literacy can ever account for the various ways literacy is practiced, valued, or described. Most ways of defining literacy, Scribner (1984) asserts, assume literacy has an "essence" that can be defined and described (7). However, as Scribner states and this study confirms, literacy is "a many-meaninged thing" (9).

While there is no one "thing" we can call *literacy*, there are multiple *views* of what literacy should be, all with their own agendas and "rationalizations of . . . [literacy's] importance" (Knoblauch 1990, 74–75). To put it another way, questions of what literacy *is* are invariably questions of what literacy *should be*. Ways of seeing literacy are always ideological in that they are reflections of the worldviews of individuals and groups and always political in that they privilege certain groups or literacy practices while marginalizing or excluding others.

I define a *conception of literacy* as a set of values and beliefs about literacy that colors one's way of viewing language and, consequently, the world. It is, to use Kenneth Burke's (1966) term, a "terministic screen" that consists of the set of symbols we have for interpreting the world. Burke (1966) argues that we do not experience reality directly, that, rather, our sense of it is always mediated by language, which itself is a "*reflection* of reality" we use for "*selection*" and "*deflection*" (45; emphasis in original). A terministic screen always involves an element of sifting through, of choosing certain ideas or experiences and deflecting others. Burke says one's terministic screen necessarily "directs the attention to one field [of language] rather than another" (50).

Similarly, a conception of literacy directs our attention to particular *dimensions* of literacy rather than to others. By *dimensions*, I mean aspects of the literacy, including the self or the individual, the social dimension, the text, and production. Two individuals viewing the same literacy event might come to very different conclusions about the event depending on the dimensions of literacy privileged in their conception. A conception, then, is a way of choosing, consciously or not, certain aspects of our experiences with language.

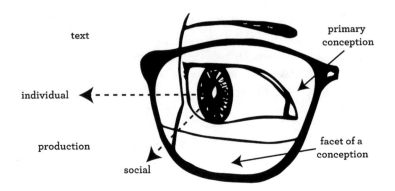

text

primary
conception

individual

production

facet of a
conception

social

Figure 1.1. A conception of literacy

Although I like Burke's metaphor of the screen, I also think it needs updating given that we now gaze primarily *at* screens rather than *through* them. Consequently, I see a conception as a lens, similar to a bifocal or trifocal lens, in which the subject gazes mostly through their primary literacy conception but, depending on the situation, might also look through another part of the lens, which could represent another literacy *facet*. In figure 1.1, I depict a conception of literacy as a bifocal lens, which, when the individual gazes through it, sorts the viewer's attention to particular dimensions of literacy. For example, a viewer could see mostly how literacy can act as a vehicle for self-expression while not paying as much attention to how relationships (the social dimension) or texts enable this journey.

As with any literacy educator, when new graduate instructors profess literacy, they make choices about what to teach and how to teach it, choices that reflect their ideas and attitudes about what literacy is and who and what it is for. Graduate instructors are influenced by the kinds of texts (written, visual, aural, and electronic) they read, as well as familial and cultural literacy practices, current and prior experiences in school, and cultural commonplaces about literacy. These in turn influence the literacy practices they value and want to see replicated. In one of his continuations of Deborah Brandt's (1998) theory of literacy sponsorship, Eli Goldblatt (2007) argues that "the more we know about where our students come from and what the literacy conditions are around our institution, the better chance we have of designing a program that truly fits our environment" (9). I argue that this is no less true of the graduate instructors we educate and the practica we design.

FROM LITERACY DEFINITIONS TO CONCEPTIONS

All scholarship dealing with literacy defines it, even if the definitions are implicit. However, only a few scholars have made explicit attempts to classify different views of literacy. James Berlin's (1982) taxonomies, particularly his "current-traditional rhetoric," have been the most influential in the field of composition. However, the most recent work on mapping the landscape of literacy views comes from Peter Goggin (2008), who articulates the most detailed synthesis of different literacy views. Although the corpus he is using is much different from this study's,[6] based on my past experiences with teacher education, this taxonomy makes the most sense as a starting point for understanding the views of new graduate instructors.

In the following descriptions, I also refer to overlapping classifications of literacy forwarded by two other scholars: psychologist Sylvia Scribner (1984) and compositionist C. H. Knoblauch (1990), both of whom Goggin cites in formulating his literacy categories.[7]

1. Functionalist Literacy

The most familiar way of conceptualizing literacy in the public sphere is what Knoblauch (1990) and Goggin (2008) term the *functionalist perspective*. Functionalist-literacy views see literacy primarily in terms of its practical value. Also termed *vocational literacy*, this conception argues for the necessity of equipping people with the literacy skills needed to survive in daily life (Scribner 1984, 9). This view, Knoblauch (1990) says, presumes "that the ultimate value of language lies in its utilitarian capacity to pass information back and forth for economic or other material gain" (76). In other words, this literacy view assumes literacy does, in fact, have an essence or some set of basic skills that can be taught in a relatively straightforward way.

2. Instrumental Literacy

Goggin (2008) also adds a twin classification to functionalist that he calls "functional literacy," which is, in his view, a more "reflective and critical" approach to literacy that attends to functional concerns while still maintaining "a multiliteracy view in which the acquisition of discrete learning skills can contribute to various forms of learning" (72). Though still practical, this view sees literacy as context based, flexible, and multimodal. Before I began gathering data, I renamed the functional literacy category *instrumental literacy* in order to prevent confusion between this and the functionalist view. Here I draw on Durst's (1999) concept of "reflexive instrumentalism," which he describes as accepting the practical goals of literacy instruction by recognizing the importance of "the world of work and career advancement" while also preserving "the intellectual rigor and social analysis of current [critical] pedagogies" (174, 178). This conception, then, "cultivate[s] a critical aspect within this instrumentalist framework" (178).

3. Social/Critical Literacy

Social/critical literacy sees literacy as socially situated and ideological (Goggin 2008, 70). Literacy in this view is a vehicle for social uplift, community advancement, and questioning existing power structures. Citing Paulo Freire, Scribner (1984) describes this conception as one that looks to literacy "as a means for poor and politically powerless groups to claim their place in the world" (12). In other words, literacy, in this conception, is a means for analyzing one's condition through what Freire calls "'critical consciousness'" in order to engage in fundamental social transformation (quoted in Scribner 1984, 12). This conception can be seen as a dangerous one because of its goal of disrupting the status quo (Knoblauch 1990, 79). However, because of composition's acceptance of challenging hierarchy as part of our mission, this conception has become relatively mainstream to scholars of composition.[8] In recognition of the strong pull of this and other social views of literacy within composition studies, Goggin adds two more categories to Knoblauch's and Scribner's classifications, both of which view literacy as social and context based: critical-activism literacy and literacy for social growth.

4. Critical Activism Literacy

Critical-activism literacy is, for Goggin (2008), a more specific classification of social/critical literacy; Goggin argues that "a literacy of critical activism will bring about radical political reform" (69). The difference between this and social/critical literacy is primarily in praxis. I interpret critical-activism literacy and social/critical literacy as occupying the same ideological category or as existing on a continuum, with critical-activism literacy emphasizing a higher degree of community involvement and requiring students to take part in their community rather than just writing to respond to social and community issues.

5. Literacy for Social Growth

Like social/critical and critical-activism literacy, literacy for social growth emphasizes social construction. Unlike the other two social categories, it "tends to avoid direct activism and maintains the status quo by creating an illusion of self/social determinism" (Goggin 2008, 68). Carol Jago's (2009) work, which cites the transformative power of reading literature and argues that it lets students in on the common web of human experience, aligns with this view. Literacy, in this conception, is about connection and empathy, but the political, ideological aspects of literacy are downplayed.

6. Cultural Literacy

Scribner (1984) describes cultural literacy (which she calls "literacy as a state of grace") as "the tendency in many societies to endow the literate person with special virtues" (13). To be literate, in this conception, is to exist in a special sphere of society. Central to this conception is, as Scribner (1984) relates, "the concern with preserving and understanding scripture . . . at the core of many religious traditions, Western and non-Western alike" (13). Scribner's connection between this tendency to endow the literate person with a certain almost religious aura and the emphasis on scripture, or, what I call more broadly *the text*, provides a way for understanding views of literacy that endow even secular texts with sacred qualities.

In Knoblauch's (1990) description of cultural literacy, he foregrounds the view of language as "a repository of cultural values and to that extent a source of social cohesion" (77). Like literacy for social growth, this conception sees literacy as social, but unlike the social visions of literacy, which allow for multiple views and multiple literacies, cultural literacy strives for a unified culture. Using Knoblauch's characterization of this conception and E.D. Hirsch as the exemplar, Goggin (2008) agrees that cultural literacy is "an ideology that conceives certain texts as having stable and timeless values" (68).

7. Literacy for Personal Growth

With its emphasis on Romantic views of language, the poet-writer, and the composing process, literacy for personal growth is the conception of literacy most oriented to the individual. Knoblauch (1990) characterizes this conception by saying, "The assumption of a literacy-for-personal-growth argument is that language expresses the power of the individual imagination" (78). Consequently, adherents of this conception advocate, in some cases, "expressive writing, personalized reading programs, whole-language curricula, and open classrooms" as "symbols of self-determination" (78). Writing, in this view, is depicted "as a mysterious process and a means to an internal truth" (Goggin 2008, 67).

GRADUATE INSTRUCTORS' CONCEPTIONS OF LITERACY

While I used all seven categories for my initial coding, only three were meaningful categories for describing the participants' conceptions of literacy: literacy for personal growth, social/critical literacy, and cultural literacy. Although I coded some data for functionalist and instrumental literacy conceptions, neither was a primary conception of literacy for any of the focal participants. I can't be sure, but this could be because of an ambivalence towards language instruction, as well as a suspicion of overtly or narrowly careerist notions of literacy. That is, they all saw literacy as being *for* something else, whether it was self-expression, critical engagement with the world, or knowledge of texts. They consequently framed the purpose of education, and literacy, in much different terms than do policymakers in the public sphere, pointing to a significant difference between what outsiders expect students to learn and what is actually going on in the classroom. I note this here because, while I do not devote a chapter to them, functionalist and instrumental conceptions of literacy can often seem like the soup WPAs and literacy educators are swimming in.

Besides social/critical literacy, the other two social categories (literacy for social growth and critical-activist literacy) were also not as useful in understanding the graduate instructors' conceptions. While some graduate instructors were intrigued by critical-activist views, most saw liberatory, community-based pedagogies as unrealistic or too burdensome for their students.[9] Literacy for social growth had too many overlaps with other conceptions (especially, surprisingly, cultural literacy). Although the idea that literacy helps individuals develop empathy was intriguing for one graduate instructor, her desire to help students question existing power structures and language's role in gatekeeping made the social/critical category more descriptive of her views.

While Scribner (1984) and others have described literacy conceptions in connection with ethnographic research on literacy, this study is the first to use the conceptions I describe as a heuristic for understanding case studies of individuals, thus providing an opportunity to see how individual conceptions map onto (or reject) broader cultural understandings of literacy's purpose, as well as how experiences and sponsors communicate and/or influence how individual conceptions of literacy develop. In applying Goggin's (2008) categories, I thus bring together two previously disparate sets of scholarship: graduate-instructor education and literacy taxonomies.

However, I am sensitive to critiques by Lisa Ede (2004) and David Gold (2012), who argue there is danger in taxonomizing the paradigms of our field, particularly when they are used to place scholars into opposing camps. As Ede (2004) states, quoting feminist scholar Donna Haraway, taxonomies tend to "'police deviation,'" a serious danger when it comes to applying what we learn from studies like this to people we are educating (26). Ede thus argues that when we speak for others, we must take care not to overgeneralize, oversimplify, and decontextualize (169–71). Moreover, individuals' conceptions are enormously complex, influenced by various literacy sponsors and taking on different meanings according to context. Goggin (2008) recognizes the inherent hybridity of these conceptions in his study, pointing to the "fuzziness and leakiness of classification" (76). Because literacy sponsors come in the form of various individuals and institutions, each graduate instructor's conception of literacy was not only complex but also situationally dependent. Graduate instructors' literacy conceptions are, to use Restaino's (2012) words, the result of a "complex knot of competing and interlocked factors" (118). Thus, I saw the conceptions-of-literacy framework not as all-determining but rather as a heuristic device for making sense of the ingrained, complex views of these newcomers.

To honor this complexity whenever possible, I also read against the grain of the patterns I discovered in the data for each graduate-instructor participant, pointing to instances of complexity and hybridity. At the same time, I also make the case that each of the graduate instructors had one *primary conception*, which acted as a lens through which every other conception was viewed and filtered. In calling this a *primary conception*, I invoke

James Paul Gee's (1989) idea of a primary discourse because I see the primary conception as constituting part of what Gee calls our "home-based sense of identity" (8).[10] This primary conception functioned as the graduate instructors' terministic screen for viewing literacy, and, in some cases, it also limited their ability to enact practices based on other conceptions. For example, Jordi, a third-year PhD student in literature, was intrigued by and used many of the pedagogical strategies presented in the practicum, including small-group work and collaborative, constructive activities aimed at helping students interpret texts by interacting with them. However, the way she viewed literacy was inflected by her primary conception, cultural literacy, in her understanding that literacy was primarily about interpreting texts. Consequently, although Jordi frequently referred to what might be described as *social/critical literacy goals*, goals that students develop an awareness of texts as ideological and have knowledge of current events, she had difficulty pinpointing *why* students should develop this awareness other than that it would help them interpret texts.

Of course, as Shirley Brice Heath and Brian Street (2008) argue, "*Why* questions are teleological in nature and resist proof by empirical means" (35). It is thus understandable that Jordi, a newcomer to teaching, would have difficulty articulating the basis for beliefs that have become so naturalized for her they no longer seem to *be* beliefs. Thus, even as I posit that, in Burkean terms, graduate instructors' conceptions redirect their gaze to only certain aspects of the literacy experience, I also recognize and point to how their views and experiences could and did work as strengths. The goal of practica instructors should thus be not to work against graduate instructors' literacy views, which would surely backfire, as work by Welch (1993) and Jackie Grutsch McKinney and Elizabeth Chiseri-Strater (2003) also confirms (Grutsch McKinney and Chiseri-Strater 2003). Rather, practica instructors can create situations that help new graduate instructors understand and denaturalize their conceptions of literacy, creating opportunities for them to examine how these belief systems inform their teaching practices.

IDENTITY AND RESISTANCE IN THE EDUCATION
OF COLLEGE WRITING INSTRUCTORS

The conceptions-of-literacy framework described here also offers new ways of seeing the impact of two often-discussed aspects of graduate-teacher education: identity and resistance. As recent studies by Grouling (2015) and Rachel Gramer (2017) attest, graduate instructor "resistance" to aspects of their early teacher education has become somewhat an overdetermining narrative in the field. To name but a few, Hesse (1993) argues that graduate instructors "resisted material that was new" and, as a result, could not engage with it (225). Rankin (1994) concurs that her first-year graduate instructors "resist almost everything" and are particularly against the "theory" presented in the practicum course (ix, 45). Ebest (2005) and Barb Blakely Duffelmeyer (2005) both take up the subject of graduate-student resistance to specific aspects of the practicum course (e.g., decentered classrooms and critical pedagogy). Indeed, resistance has become such a well-established aspect of graduate instructors' early experiences with teaching and pedagogy that Dryer (2012) states that their "resistance to the practicum may be a given" (423).

I should point out that resistance in the practicum isn't always constructed as negative or as an impediment. Articles by Welch (1993) and Marcy Taylor and Jennifer Holberg (1999) locate graduate instructors' resistance in their liminal position within the university, arguing against models based on indoctrinating or converting graduate instructors to a particular set of theoretical beliefs and practices (Taylor and Holberg 1999). Whereas studies by Bishop (1990), Farris (1996), and Ebest (2005) look to ways of overcoming graduate instructors' resistance, Welch (1993) and Estrem and Reid (2012) explore ways it can be potentially productive.

I witnessed instances when the required curriculum of the FYWP and the recommended pedagogical strategies of the graduate practicum seemed at odds with what these new graduate instructors wanted to teach. However, I argue against framing this struggle as *resistance*, which has become a catchall term for everything from outright rebellion to quiet noncompliance. The moments the graduate instructors in this study seemed most "resistant" centered around instances in which they were encountering difficulty in making sense of a particular pedagogical theory or theorist. What has been described as *resistance*, then, may in fact be moments when graduate instructors are grappling with what Linda Adler-Kassner and Elizabeth Wardle (2015) call "threshold concepts," or ideas many composition theorists have accepted but that appear to go against the common sense articulated by people outside the discipline (Adler-Kassner and Wardle 2015, xix). This view supports Reid, Estrem, and Belcheir's (2012) conclusion that the "resistance" we see in graduate practica "may be more inertial than consciously directed" and that it stems from graduate instructors' interaction with the "least familiar" of the "new-and-complicated ideas" they are exposed to in their practica (55). I agree with Reid, Estrem, and Belcheir, with the slight modification that the ideas new graduate instructors find most troubling are the ones that run counter to their conceptions of literacy. Revising this narrative of resistance, which has dominated scholarship on graduate-teacher education, may help WPAs and practica instructors be more empathetic to and understanding of the struggles graduate instructors face in their first year of teaching.

Thus, this book redirects our focus from resistance to the ideological positions of the graduate instructors. If, as theorists like George Hillocks (1995), Berlin (1982), and Wardle (2014) point out, our theories of language and literacy, and of who and what constitutes literacy, impact *who* we are and become as teachers, it becomes essential for graduate-teacher education to provide inroads for new graduate instructors that help them uncover their literacy conceptions.

Although past studies (Dobrin 2005; Ebest 2005; Welch 1993) have pointed to the ideology and identity-changing nature of the practicum course, my analysis suggests, along with recent studies by Dryer (2012) and Reid, Estrem, and Belcheir (2012), that the practicum course has limited and uneven effects on graduate instructors' identities and pedagogy. Dobrin

(2005), for example, ascribes a great deal of power to the practicum course.

> We must recognize that the manner in which the practicum disseminates cultural capital is a means of control. . . . By professing a particular cultural capital through the practicum, the program itself is able to maintain control over what can and should be taught not just in FYC classes but also in any other class students then teach. (25)

However, one of the findings of the study informing this book is that the conceptions of literacy the graduate instructors brought with them to their first semester of teaching were both persistent, even in the face of competing ideas about literacy from the practicum, and influential on what got taught in the individual composition courses. Thus, throughout this book, I question the idea that the practicum has the power to "maintain control" over what graduate instructors choose to teach and/or how they teach it.

This is not to say graduate instructors are either uneducable or deficit laden because they do not enter teaching methods classes as blank slates. Indeed, the conceptions-of-literacy framework points to understanding graduate-instructor "resistance" not in terms of stubbornness or rebellion but rather the very real and understandable challenges new graduate instructors face and what we (as teacher educators) can do to support them. The graduate instructors I profile here grew up in households that valued certain literacies, which were then reinforced by various literacy sponsors throughout their education, including, in some cases, other courses in their current and past graduate programs. It is thus understandable that they would persist with these literacy views. In addition, I argue, along with Gramer (2017), that graduate instructors' conceptions of literacy (she uses the term "identities") are "*enabling* as well as constraining, generative as well as limiting" (5). To return to Burke's (1966) terms, as terministic screens, conceptions of literacy enable graduate instructors to see some possibilities when it comes to teaching, writing, and their students' abilities while deflecting others. Throughout this book, I try to balance literature that has seen graduate instructors largely in terms of deficit. To do that,

I point to aspects of their conceptions of literacy that strengthened rather than detracted from their pedagogy. The data from this study suggest the practicum *did* have an influence over the graduate instructors in that they appeared to be more conscious of and critical of their own literacy positions and prejudices by the end of the first semester. Although this was just the beginning of a process through which graduate instructors interrogated their literacy positions and started to make sense of what those positions meant for their teaching practices, it reveals the possibilities for the practicum's role in their development as teachers. However, the role of the practicum in graduate instructors' teaching trajectories is neither straightforward nor necessarily easy to see. In many ways, the practicum's influence wasn't as pronounced (and as recognizable) as other sources of learning for the graduate instructors, including past experiences, familial values, and even other graduate programs or other forces within their graduate program. While learning and reflection in the graduate practicum are possible, they are always inflected by past experiences and beliefs and may take longer than a single semester to solidify. Moreover, graduate instructors also must be willing to commit to the kind of intense self-exploration this learning entails.

GRADUATE INSTRUCTORS AND RESEARCH ON LEARNING: IMPLICATIONS FOR WORK ON TRANSFER

Looking at the learning trajectories of new graduate instructors also has implications for recent work in composition on student learning, which is often framed in terms of theories of transfer. Arguing that students' "prior knowledge . . . [and conceptions of literacy] plays a decisive if not determining role in . . . [their] successful transfer of writing knowledge and practice," Kathleen Blake Yancey, Liane Robertson, and Kara Taczak (2014) describe three different transfer practices learners use in encountering new tasks:

1. An *assemblage* model in which students graft new . . . knowledge onto earlier understandings

2. A more successful *remix* model in which students integrate prior and new writing knowledge

3. A *critical incident* model where students encounter an obstacle that helps them retheorize writing in general (5)

As the descriptions above indicate, Yancey, Robertson and Taczak see the remix and critical incident models of learning to be more successful, as they enable students, more so than in the assemblage model, to retheorize writing. Yet I argue that for graduate instructors in their first semester to first year of teaching, assemblage may be a more realistic model. For the most part, when the graduate instructors referred to ideas and practices they learned in the practicum, those ideas and practices were grafted onto previous understandings without significantly altering those understandings. This supports Estrem and Reid's (2012) claim that for new graduate instructors, "new learning does not replace earlier learning as much as it synthesizes with earlier understandings, sometimes wholly and sometimes partially, attaching readily when new and old principles match and perhaps less strongly when there are conflicting principles" (462).

Given the power of their literacy preconceptions and the difficult and often counterintuitive nature of writing pedagogy, I don't think we can expect graduate instructors to do much retheorizing in the space of a single semester, although it does appear that some of those grafted-on understandings eventually work their way into graduate instructors' conceptions of literacy once they have had the chance to consider those understandings more completely and gain additional teaching practice. I do, however, note moments when a critical incident forced a situation in which the graduate instructors began to question and retheorize more thoroughly. For example, her struggle with one of her seminar papers prompted Karen, a comp/ rhet graduate instructor, to rethink how the experiences of her undergraduates might parallel her own, a relationship she had previously effaced.

One of the main feats of Yancey, Robertson, and Taczak's (2014) study, as well as other recent work on transfer, has been to acknowledge and identify the role of *prior knowledge* in students' learning. For example, Mary Jo Reiff and Anis Bawarshi (2011) argue that although there has been increasing focus on how students in FYCs transfer their knowledge to other contexts, there has been relatively little research on what students bring with them to the course (313). My argument is essentially the same, but applied to graduate instructors. In other words, understanding the conceptions of literacy graduate instructors bring with them to their first semester of teaching might help explain how they take in pedagogy and rethink prior views (see also Qualley 2016).

However, I also think that in labeling what students bring with them to their learning as *knowledge* (as research on transfer often does), we might continue to underestimate its impact. For example, Yancey, Robertson, and Taczak (2014) argue that "prior *knowledge* . . . plays a decisive if not determining role in students' successful transfer of writing *knowledge* and practice" (5; emphasis mine). By viewing knowledge as imbedded in or interacting with *worldviews,* we might gain a more complete picture of why new graduate instructors sometimes resist new information when it is not consistent with these worldviews. To put it another way, it's not simply what graduate instructors know but the attitudes, beliefs, and behaviors they associate with this knowing. *Knowledge* is almost too neutral a term for the beliefs graduate instructors (and others) bring with them to their learning.

Scholars have also begun to question the use of the term *transfer* as helpful in understanding students' learning trajectories. In a panel on transfer at CCCC 2018, Elizabeth Wardle stated that "we should stop talking about transfer," explaining that while it is a useful shorthand, what we are often talking about are "complex transitions, repurposing, and generalizing" (Downs, Moore, and Ringer 2018). Moreover, Danica Schieber (2016) argues that much of the learning students bring with them from one situation into the next is "invisible to both themselves and their . . . instructors" because once learning has taken place, students no longer recognize what they have learned *as* something learned; it becomes naturalized (464).

This research complicates efforts to see how much graduate instructors learn from their graduate practica courses, as well as from other informal and formal sites of pedagogy education. However, I also think a potential way in is to tell more complex stories that might account for how graduate instructors' literacy experiences complicate, enrich, or make visible or invisible their learning trajectories as new teachers. Thus, I hope the case studies I present in the following chapters productively challenge work on learning by bringing graduate instructors' preconceptions to the fore and demonstrating how significant they are as the graduate instructors take up the concepts presented to them in their practica.

CHAPTER OVERVIEW

In order to highlight the importance of graduate instructors' conceptions of literacy in determining how they take in and interact with pedagogy, in the next three chapters, I present case studies of new graduate instructors, organized according to the following conceptions of literacy: literacy for personal growth, cultural literacy, and social/critical literacy. In chapter 2, "Yoga Ashrams and Mother-Teachers: Literacy for Personal Growth," I discuss this most individually oriented conception. In this chapter, I present case studies of Lily and Karen, the two graduate instructors whose field was composition and rhetoric. Through these case studies, I examine how their beliefs, including the idea that reading and writing are "natural" processes that happen best when teachers get out of the way, both guided and (in some cases) limited them in terms of the possibilities they saw for teaching in their first semester. I end this chapter by examining how we can best support graduate instructors who hold similar views, including ways to work within potential tensions between these beliefs and composition theory.

Chapter 3, "Texts, Hierarchy, and Ritual: Cultural Literacy," discusses the primacy of the text for the literature PhD students, Jordi, Garrett, and Blake, and its implications for their teaching practice. In this chapter, I argue that these three unknowingly reify a problematic distinction between their students' writing and other "higher" texts. I also discuss how they seemed to view literacy in terms of ritual, imbuing a quasi-religious quality to texts and describing their own initiation into academia in religious terms. As in previous chapters, I analyze how these conceptions influenced their teaching, drawing connections between their tendency to focus on readings as opposed to writing in their classrooms and their felt sense of the importance of texts.

Although cultural literacy and literacy for personal growth appear to reflect commonplaces about literacy within our larger culture, social/critical ways of viewing literacy are largely alien to newcomers to the fields comprising English studies. This is the focus of chapter 4, "Graduate Instructors at the Threshold: Threshold Concepts, Disciplinarity, and Social/ Critical Literacy," which examines the graduate instructors' initiation into the discourse of composition theory, with its heavy emphasis on social/critical ways of viewing literacy. In this chapter, I use the concept of threshold concepts, as well as work in composition about threshold concepts, particularly Adler-Kassner and Wardle's (2015) *Naming What We Know: Threshold Concepts of Writing Studies*. The data in this chapter support the idea that these concepts can be "troublesome knowledge," as even the graduate instructors who held social/critical views of literacy at times struggled with how to enact a pedagogy based on them (Meyer and Land 2006, 9). I use the data in this chapter to point both to the value of articulating "what we know" for compositionists and to the difficulty of using these concepts as ways into writing pedagogy for newcomers.

I hope the case studies I present are useful to practica instructors and graduate instructors alike: both might recognize themselves, their students, and their colleagues in these descriptions, giving practica instructors insight into how to encourage their graduate students' strengths and also manage the difficulties and conflicts that might arise. To that end, in the concluding chapter, I point to the implications of these findings for reconsidering best practices for educating graduate instructors.

In this chapter, I argue that the goal of the practicum course should be to help graduate instructors come to an understanding of their literacy conceptions. In particular, I discuss asking graduate instructors to write and revise an autobiographical literacy narrative as a key tool for enabling the critical self-reflection needed to create a purposeful pedagogy.

2

YOGA ASHRAMS AND MOTHER-TEACHERS
Literacy for Personal Growth

Sometimes when someone speaks or writes about something that is very important to him [sic], the words he produces have this striking integration or coherence: he isn't having to plan and work them out one by one. . . . The meanings have been blended at a finer level, integrated more thoroughly. Not merely manipulated by his mind, but, rather, sifted through his entire self. In such writing you don't feel mechanical cranking, you don't hear the gears change. When there are transitions they are smooth, natural, organic. It is as though every word is permeated by the meaning of the whole.

—Peter Elbow

Models of composing that highlight the individual dimension of literacy characterized much of the early work in the field of composition as it was taking shape in the 1960s and 1970s. Within composition, a focus on what individuals actually did as they composed gave birth to the process movement, which continues to shape pedagogy in composition and related fields today. In addition, views of the writer as autonomous and agentive and as striving for both a unifying truth and individual recognition have become a cultural motif, prevalent not just within English departments and creative writing camps, where they remain attractive reasons for devoting a life to writing, but also in conceptions of literacy in society at large.

Despite composition's origins, many of the terms and ideas associated with what I call the *literacy-for-personal-growth*

DOI: 10.7330/9781607329343.c002

conception are no longer by themselves sufficient ways of characterizing writing and the first-year classroom in composition theory. Terms like *natural, growth, voice,* and *authenticity,* located in the early work of the so-called expressivists, scholars like Peter Elbow, Donald M. Murray, and Wendy Bishop, were questioned and critiqued in the response to expressivism and process in the 1980s by social constructivist figures like Kenneth Bruffee (1984) and Bartholomae (1995). Although ideas associated with expressivism are enjoying a resurgence, to the extent that scholars are beginning to investigate possible intersections between expressivist and critical pedagogy,[1] many composition scholars have deemed ideas associated with literacy for personal growth problematic because they do not recognize the social, situated, and rhetorical nature of literacy. For example, counter to the Elbow's (1998) description of writing in the epigraph at the beginning of this chapter, the recognition that writing is not, in fact, "natural," is one of the threshold concepts included in Adler-Kassner and Wardle's (2015) *Naming What We Know* (27).

Past research in the area of teacher education has not discussed literacy for personal growth per se, but the influence of this conception on the cohorts of graduate instructors these researchers studied is evident. Indeed, though not often identified as such, literacy for personal growth appears to be the conception authors of past studies of graduate-instructor education remark upon the most. Bishop (1990), for example, describes one of the participants in her study as having "more than a touch of . . . a romantic devotion to the image of the individual writer" (81). Similarly, in their now iconic "Conventions, Conversations, and the Writer: Case Study of a Student in a Rhetoric Ph.D. Program," Carol Berkenkotter, Thomas Huckin, and John Ackerman (1988) introduce Nate, a graduate student whose view that "writers have a 'personal voice'" was "central to his teaching philosophy" (10).

These studies forecast the possibility that writing program administrators, practicum instructors, and mentors whose field is composition studies may be discomfited when encountering these views in graduate instructors. Cole and Lyon (2008) note "romantic notions of creativity and genius" as one of a few "problematic ideologies" new graduate students may bring with them to their teacher-preparation course (194–95). Rankin (1994) argues that two of the graduate instructors in her study are so committed to the concept of finding their own voice and helping students locate theirs that they are "not able, or perhaps not ready, to hear the voices of others" (65). Berkenkotter, Huckin, and Ackerman's (1988) Nate also encounters problems because of his commitment to the idea of voice, particularly when it comes to writing in the initially alien field of rhetoric and composition.

My interpretation of the data I collected confirms that literacy for personal growth may be a problematic conception for new graduate instructors, particularly if they implicitly believe composition courses can't foster "real" writing (which isn't learned or learnable but inspired). In particular, Lily and Karen, despite their backgrounds in education, saw teachers as getting in the way of what they viewed as students' natural ability and love for reading and writing, a belief that in some ways blocked their ability to invest in and develop strategies to help students analyze and produce new kinds of texts. However, as with any conception of literacy, this view was both enabling and constraining in that while it limited their ways of seeing literacy in some ways, it also enabled them to identify with the struggles of students who weren't feeling personally invested in their writing and to create strategies to increase student interest.

Moreover, I argue that if new graduate instructors are given the tools to critically examine literacy for personal growth, individual views of literacy have the potential to act in conjunction with more critical, contextual understandings. In order to demonstrate this possibility, in this chapter I discuss Lily and Karen, the graduate instructors whose primary conception was literacy for personal growth, and, surprisingly, who were the two graduate instructors whose field was rhetoric and composition.

DEFINING LITERACY FOR PERSONAL GROWTH IN
THE CONTEXT OF GRADUATE-INSTRUCTOR VIEWS

In Goggin's (2008) classification system, "literacy for personal growth" views are characterized by their emphasis on the mystery of the composing process, as well as its role in helping individuals pursue "internal truth" (67). This conception views literacy as valuable for individuals because it enables personal fulfillment and attainment. As in some early expressivist work, school, and particularly what are viewed as overly mechanical or form-based assignments, is depicted as getting in the way of this development. The graduate instructors who held this view differentiated the reading they did for pleasure from academic reading; they elevated reading for pleasure and also tended to depict reading and writing as largely solitary and individual.

A pedagogy based on personal growth may emphasize the needs of individual learners, encouraging teachers to institute programs geared to individual student interests, such as personalized reading programs that let students either select their own texts or have options geared to different interests. The two graduate instructors I discuss in this chapter both described moments in which they were not free to choose what they read or wrote about, which they associated with stifling the self-examination they saw as the goal of literacy.

Literacy for personal growth was a pervasive conception of literacy among the participants. I assigned this code to more segments of data than any other single code, with 355 total codes representing literacy for personal growth compared to 274 for social/critical literacy, the next largest category.[2] Even though I anticipated I would find the conception of literacy for personal growth to some extent given the omnipresence of personal-growth conceptions of composing in US society, its frequency in the data was surprising.

In table 2.1 below, I use counts for the literacy for personal growth code (from the qualitative-data-management software Atlas.ti) to indicate what percentage of each participant's total codes this code comprised, giving me a sense of which participants were most influenced by this conception.

Table 2.1. Numbers for literacy for personal growth, as a ratio and a percentage of each focal participant's total codes

Participant	Discipline	Ratio of PG codes to participants' total codes	Percentage of PG codes
Lily	comp/rhet	145/210	69.0
Karen	comp/rhet	50/101	49.5
Barbara	creative writing	50/143	35.0
Max	creative writing	30/104	28.9
Garrett	literature	25/104	24.0
Jordi	literature	31/167	18.6
Blake	literature	13/111	11.7

The participants who were most aligned with this conception of literacy were Lily and Karen, the two comp/rhet graduate students. The ubiquity of this conception not only in my data but also in studies by others doing work in the area of teacher education (Berkenkotter, Huckin, and Ackerman 1988; Bishop 1990; Ebest 2005; Rankin 1994) suggests many new comp/rhet students could come to graduate school not really knowing the social/critical emphasis more current in the field. This makes sense in that until recently, composition and rhetoric has not been considered an area of study for undergraduates. Given the prevalence of personal-growth understandings of literacy in US culture, I expect that even with more English departments and independent writing and rhetoric departments offering a major in composition and rhetoric, practicum instructors might continue to see graduate instructors who are drawn to teaching writing because they value personal expression.

In the early literacy narratives, I counted twenty-five content units representing literacy for personal growth, spread over five of the seven participants: Lily, Barbara, Jordi, Garrett, and Karen. Given the association of personal models of composing and women's work, it is noteworthy that the only male participant who had codes for this conception of literacy in the first draft of his narrative was Garrett, and all these moments associate his view of literacy with a woman, his grandmother (pers.

comm. September 10, 2010). I say this not to suggest it is more likely for women to hold these views but rather to demonstrate how this view has been gendered, especially in depictions of composition instruction as women's work (see Schell 1998). Moreover, some aspects of literacy for personal growth, such as the use of personal narrative (particularly in academic writing), can be associated more with women's composing, even though personal narrative itself is not gender specific (see Enos 2003).

In the revised narratives turned in at the end of the semester, codes for literacy for personal growth showed up among all the participants, suggesting that the more social and critical composition theory presented in the practicum did not extinguish personal-growth ways of viewing writing. Indeed, whereas I would have expected the social/critical emphasis to lessen the extent to which personal-growth ideas showed up in the revised narratives, Lily's and Karen's narratives expanded upon stories illustrating ideas like *writing is something not to be interfered with* or *writing is about finding oneself.*

In the remainder of this chapter, I use Lily's and Karen's interviews and literacy narratives to describe their conceptions of literacy in depth. I begin by giving brief bios of Lily and Karen, using data from their interviews and literacy narratives to describe the sponsors and experiences that shaped their conceptions of literacy. I then conduct a closer examination of Lily's and Karen's literacy narratives because both followed similar trajectories in which they reject authoritarian teaching and "canned" curricula to pursue more nurturing teaching identities. Finally, I turn to how personal-growth conceptions of literacy translated into their teaching, describing my observations of two of their classes, one in the fall and one in the following spring. To conclude the chapter, I discuss how the practicum created (and could also do a better job of creating) a space where they could begin to analyze and revise their literacy conceptions.

Before I turn to this data, I should note some conscious decisions I made about how to tell Lily's and Karen's stories, as well as my own stance on their literacy perspectives. Like many scholars in composition and rhetoric, I have been socialized to see literacy through the lens of social and rhetorical assumptions. So while I agree with Ede (2004) that there is danger in treating, for example, process and social-epistemic theories of literacy as fundamentally separate, I also think we must push back on some of the more problematic assumptions behind *some* expressivist views, such as the idea that writing is natural, that it can't be taught, or that it shouldn't be too formulaic.

I note here too that as straight, cisgender, white women, Lily and Karen may not have had some of the experiences that would allow them to view singular or "authentic" constructions of voice, for example, more critically. As Jacqueline Jones Royster (1996) argues, and more recent work by Carmen Kynard (2015) reminds us, people of color have always had to think strategically about how they deploy different voices, and people who identify as queer may also have more complex understandings of voice (see Waite 2016). I say this not to essentialize either Lily or Karen or to suggest that having a concept of an authentic voice was somehow a personal shortcoming. Rather, it is one of the limitations of my study and of the graduate program and practicum course at its center that we did not have more diverse representation that might have helped us, as a group, launch a fuller critique of singular conceptions of voice or naturalized understandings of writing and language.

I also think there is danger in communicating to new graduate instructors that we don't value their initial perspectives and experiences or that they have no place in our current pedagogy. Recognizing that Lily and Karen are newcomers to composition pedagogy, I hold back on criticizing their perspectives or teaching as I describe them. I also considered putting words like *natural* in quotes but felt that, while it might work in some places, to do this every time would feel too judgmental of two new teachers who gave me the great gift of their time as I conducted this study. As I mention earlier, Lily and Karen were both gifted teachers who cared about their students and who strove to create classes where students felt heard and where they could make meaningful connections to their writing.

Lily and Karen: Literacy Sponsors and Conceptions

As a first-year PhD student in her midtwenties, Lily gave off a mix of enthusiasm and trepidation that belied her prior experiences with teaching and tutoring. Lily attended a public high school in a suburban area close to Public U. She went to college at a private, liberal arts school and finally attended a well-known school of education, also in the Northeast. After she earned her master's degree, she started teaching high-school English but found it wasn't for her. She described this briefly in her interview, saying, "I guess I just felt like I wanted to do more of my own reading and writing. And have more me time" (pers. comm., October 15, 2010). Pursuing a doctoral degree in English was consequently an immensely personal quest in that she was looking to it as an opportunity for self-exploration.

Lily was a devout student of yoga having lived at a yoga ashram for six months, an experience she describes as "life changing" ("Literacy Narrative Draft," 2010). According to Lily,

> There, I took up a writing and meditation practice where I shed, a little more, the identity I had taken on as an adolescent that labeled me a bad writer. I found that the less and less I thought about how much of an artist I really was, the more art I actually produced. . . . I had finally accessed an intelligence that I thought I had all along but perceived myself as too unmotivated to stick with it. The more interesting part, however, was that it was not intelligence or talent that I uncovered, it was more a sense of trust and worth that I could push through.

Yoga was a defining part of her that clearly transferred to her pedagogy and classroom practice. She was thrilled that the first two units on the standard syllabus focused on Gandhi's writings on nonviolence. When I asked her if she talked about yoga during these units, she replied, "Oh, yeah. Oh my god, yeah. I didn't want to talk about politics at all [*laughs*]. We just talked about the Bhagavad Gita and not being attached to the fruits of your actions. It was cool" (pers. comm., October 15, 2010). I note too how yoga, at least in this moment, transferred into a conception that writing is an ability that already exists within but that simply must be "accessed."

The most ubiquitous idea in Lily's literacy conception was authenticity. In early expressivist work and in Romantic ideology, the notions of voice and of authenticity come out of a desire that writers represent their real or true selves—what they believe, feel, and subjectively experience rather than what society tells them to think. As Lily put her desire for authenticity, which she refers to as "integrity," into the context of the composition class she was teaching, she revealed how Eastern thought influenced her conception of literacy. In this passage, Lily describes what she means by integrity, using tenets from Kripalu yoga:

> [Integrity is] being true, aligning kind of . . . what you think and what you do. What you feel. This is the Kripalu. Like, the three facets of yoga. If you align what you think, feel, do, and say, then you're more authentic in what you say. (pers. comm., October 15, 2010)

I interpreted the last part of this excerpt, in which Lily talks about the alignment of "what you think, feel, do, and say," as the cornerstone of her understanding of authenticity, and, indeed, literacy.

*   *   *

Karen, a first-year PhD student in her early forties, ended up, like Lily, specializing in composition and rhetoric, making her and Lily the only two composition and rhetoric students in a practicum class of eighteen. Unlike Lily, she did not come to the program knowing she wanted to specialize in comp/rhet and intended at first to pursue a literature focus. However, she developed a connection with David over their shared history of working with high-school students. Karen brought ten years of experience teaching at a private boarding school in a rural area to her first semester of college teaching, more than any of the other graduate instructors, some of whom sought out her guidance on pedagogy.

Because of her teaching experience, Karen, unlike many of the other participants, identified more with her teaching (rather than her student or scholarly) role. In fact, during this first semester of her graduate-school experience, Karen had trouble adjusting to the student role. During her initial interview, she portrayed graduate school as frustrating what she saw as her natural, expressive writing process. She described a creative piece about her experience of meeting her husband's family as "much easier to write" and more "interesting," saying, "I was inspired by something that I wrote down and then it came to me all at once" (pers. comm., November 19, 2010). Here, Karen's process is not only one of ease but also seems romantic and even mysterious. Her role as a writer is simply to record what comes to her.

Contrasting with this is Karen's seminar paper, which required her to adopt a new way of writing more appropriate to graduate-level work. However, Karen felt the restriction school can often impose on writing. She said,

> I wasn't excited about it. . . . It's that this class [*sighs*]. . . . I sat down, and it was like a mind dump. And then I went through it and kept cutting stuff out. I kept on refining it. And this gave me a headache writing it. . . . One of the things that made it difficult is I was assigned this topic. . . . Um, you know she [the seminar professor] didn't give us a choice; she told us what chapter we were responsible for. (pers. comm., November 19, 2010)

Central to Karen's views are the roles of school and the teacher as agents of oppression. They are imposing too many rules on Karen, to the extent that she even has a physical response. Karen also invokes one of the central tenets of early expressivist work, which is that students get to choose their own subject. Whereas creative writing (and "interesting" writing) allows her to showcase her "voice" and thus her "self," writing that is chosen for her is stifling. Karen channeled these beliefs and experiences into her teaching by creating in-class workshops to help students make their writing more interesting and giving students as much choice as possible.

Authoritarian Fathers and Mother-Teachers

In her work on literacy narratives, Kara Poe Alexander (2011) argues that students tend to draw unconsciously on literacy tropes, cultural narratives, and dominant gender myths. In their literacy narratives, both Lily and Karen invoke the commonplace of the rigid, authoritarian teacher who disrupts what they view as a natural love of literacy. In its place, both posit an alternative teacher: the nurturing mother-teacher. In essence, Karen's and Lily's narratives unknowingly recapitulate one of composition's origin stories, in which, as Elizabeth Flynn (2003) describes it, the "figure of the authoritative father [is replaced] with an image of a nurturing mother" (423). The teacher-as-nurturer view, while compelling for these two, has long been critiqued in composition not only for how it essentializes women but also because of the personal sacrifices it demands of women teachers and particularly women of color, who are cast into "institutionally inferior" positions (Ritter 2012, 402) and stripped of the authority to challenge their students (see also Jarratt 2003; Schell 1998).

Despite the problems with this narrative, in this section, I focus on potential influences on these worldviews, as well as how Lily and Karen channeled their desire not to emulate authoritarian teachers into their own teaching. That is, in order for practica teachers to disrupt such narratives, I think we need a better understanding of where these narratives come from and how they shape the motivations of the graduate instructors who tell them. For both Lily and Karen, the harm that came from what they saw as authoritarian or overly mechanical writing instruction felt very real—so real that simply telling them their idea of the alternative teacher figure, the nurturing mother, is naïve would be equally harmful.

In Lily's first literacy narrative, the authoritarian teacher figure is a professor she had her senior year of college. She describes Professor Keller as "an Austrian who grew up in Texas and greeted us in boisterous German while in cowboy boots," detailing how he arrogantly claimed the only important works of literature were ones that "contributed to a new sense of seeing the world" ("Literacy Narrative Draft," 2010). Lily goes on to discuss how this hierarchical view of texts became challenging for her in her early twenties. She recounts,

> New problems developed in my writing. I wanted to write, but at twenty-two, felt I had no original ideas to contribute to the world. . . . I felt a real paradigm shift that semester in how I thought about life. Later on, though, I felt lost, in both my reading and writing, expecting some personal transformation that resulted from a novelty in ideas.

Although Keller's ideas seemed to sway Lily, she also reacted against the implication that some texts are innately superior to others. Her fear of not measuring up was paralyzing in this instance, brought on by the presence of a professor who got in the way of her "natural way of producing words" (Elbow 1998, 6). It is in these unfortunate circumstances that Lily began to view teachers as an encumbrance on the literacy development that would take place if not for their interference.

Similarly, Karen's narrative is a story of an untroubled way of experiencing literacy—until school gets in the way of her natural ability. Karen describes her early experiences with literacy, saying,

> My first memories of writing are warm and carefree. Writing was where I could express my fanciful imaginings about talking cats and mice or the strong feelings a winter's day break brought about. . . . I remember always writing stories and poems and slipping them onto my teacher's desks, basking in the recognition and encouragement I received. Writing was not work. In fact, it was so much fun I used to regularly declare to all who would listen that I wanted to be a writer. ("Literacy Narrative Draft," 2010)

However, Karen's initial esteem for reading was frustrated when, as Karen recounts, "Phonics, the *only* reading instruction method of my 1970s elementary education, transposed the former musical flow of words into discordance." ("Literacy Narrative Draft," 2010). By the end of her first year, she was "tested for Title I" because she couldn't read. For Karen, phonics-based methods for reading got in the way of her "native ability." If literacy for Karen was organic, phonics represented the mechanical side of literacy that ground everything to a halt and prevented her from accessing the perfection that came when she could attend to her own ways of reading and writing.

Karen's narrative again touches on the disruption of school on her literacy development when she entered "Honors English" in the tenth grade:

> My teacher, Mr. Treviso, was inspiring. He loved literature and teaching and his excitement was infection. At the beginning of the year, he asked a volunteer to create a gold star where he would post the names of the students who produced the year's best compositions. Every time he returned papers, I waited with baited breath for my name to be called and placed on the star so I would be awarded with a book chosen for this man whose erudition I so admired. Time and time again the same student's names were called, never mine. It was then I started to develop writer's block; no words seemed to be good enough to satisfy the standards of my hero. ("Literacy Narrative Draft," 2010.)

The parallels between this story and Lily's description of her Austrian literature professor are noticeable. Like Lily, Karen admired the (notably male) teacher's "erudition" and was inspired by his love of literature but suffered under his impossibly high standards. In Karen's view, her natural affinity for literacy was taken away by a system that makes "smart" people feel "stupid" (Elbow 1998, xiv).

Both Karen and Lily thus portray themselves as rule breakers in rebellion against a system they see as victimizing learners by not giving them enough choice. Lily invokes breaking the rules at a job working at as a tutor at a small, urban women's college, which offered continuing-education opportunities for women who might not have traditionally had access to a college education. Discouraged by the goals of the tutoring center, which instructed her to "teach basic grammar concepts," Lily struggled to make headway with her tutees, eventually discarding the mandate that she focus on grammar ("Literacy Narrative Draft," 2010). Instead, Lily took on the role of nurturer and supporter, a role I would later see when I observed her classes.

However, Lily's final rebellion was against Professor Keller for making her feel as though her ideas could never be "original enough." She concludes,

> Writing . . . cannot just be about contributing a new idea to the world in order to be famous or rich or successful in the academy. There must always be room for more writing and more books, and as teacher, I must teach this. ("Literacy Narrative Draft," 2010)

Lily begins to see the desire to stake out one's own small piece of intellectual property as ultimately self-serving in a way she wants to go beyond. As she says in perhaps her most Elbowian moment, "Learning to write was realizing that I could all along."

Both Karen and Lily replaced the authoritarian male teachers who failed them with hopes for the kind of teacher they would like to be: teachers who heal and nurture. Karen describes her mother; the librarian who tears out the catalog card to Karen's favorite library book and gives it to her; and her first-grade teacher as "nurturing" literacy sponsors who made writing enjoyable for her ("Literacy Narrative Final," 2010). She directly connects these experiences to her own teaching identity. Throughout both her narratives, the words "nurturing," "imaginative," "creative," and "enjoyment" show up frequently. She opposes these terms to the "canned curriculum" she was forced to follow as a high-school teacher and that she hopes she will not have to continue to follow as a composition instructor.

Whereas Karen's final narrative names individuals who nurtured her literacy development, Lily focuses more on the process of *becoming* the nurturing teacher, including at many points commentary that points to both the difficulties and impossibilities of doing so. She tells the story of April, a woman she worked with in a community literacy center near Public University, describing a remarkably upbeat individual in spite of her poverty and the fact that her children had been taken away from her because of incidents related to her disabilities. Lily describes April's good-natured but ineffectual attempts to grasp what Lily was teaching her, saying,

> She arrived to her reading appointments always with energized warmth and yellowed pictures of her children to share with

me. This part of it all fit neatly into the movie I had imagined, where I helped a disabled woman with a good heart function more skillfully in the world. But I hadn't taught her to read, even a little. After another month, April's case at the center had closed and her phone was disconnected. ("Literacy Narrative Final," 2010)

In this passage, Lily tells the story we don't see in movies like *Freedom Writers*; it is what happens when our attempts at literacy instruction fail. Of course, Lily's tale can hardly be seen as hopeless—she only worked with April for a few months and results can be difficult to attain in such a short time. Lily alternates, in this final narrative, between literacy hope and literacy despair. She clearly wants to redraw the lines of literacy and illiteracy, pulling April away from the margins, or perhaps even challenge society's unquestioning push toward literacy and its gatekeeping function. Indeed, one can see how within a critical-literacy framework that recognizes the limitations of literacy agendas like the one at work in the center where Lily worked, she might use April's story to think about what centers like this can realistically accomplish. Lily says later in the narrative, "Being literate in the way that I am has opened me up/kept me going/saved my life." She regrets that literacy couldn't do the same for April.

Nevertheless, this passage also radiates self-awareness and societal critique. Lily recognizes in her final narrative that many of the teacher-as-savior narratives told not only in books and films but also in our field can be intimidating and disabling for new graduate instructors because these stories put so much onus on the teacher rather than on the larger societal structures that make teachers' work difficult or impossible. However, she is so drawn to nurturing students like Sylvia and April that she can't help but sacrifice herself to the cause of literacy. Thus, while it is important for practica instructors and WPAs to honor stories like Lily's and Karen's, which demonstrate tremendous insight into literacy's hopes and perils, in this case I think it's also important to disrupt them or use them to point to other literacy possibilities.

Karen: An Obligation to Composition and Rhetoric

Before turning to what I observed in Karen's and Lily's classrooms, I want to take a second look at Karen's revised narrative because some of her more directly stated claims contradict my interpretation that it, like her first narrative, elevates the individual within the literacy landscape. Indeed, Karen's revised narrative reads like a conversion narrative in that it appears to posit her evolution from individual to more communal, contextual conceptions of literacy. Even as she articulates what I would associate with personal, expressive views of literacy (as described earlier), she also questions these views, characterizing them as "extravagant" and "romantic" ("Literacy Narrative Final," 2010). In her conclusion, Karen writes,

> I am now primed to take on Susan Jarratt's challenge to feminists that I read about in my practicum course to conduct my composition course so that students locate personal experiences in historical and social contexts—courses that lead students to see how differences emerging from their texts and discussions have more to do with those contexts than they do with an essential and unarguable individuality. . . . [I hope to help students] argue about the ethical implications of discourse . . . [and in so doing] identify their personal interests with others, understand those interests as implicated in a larger communal setting, and advance them in a public voice.

Here, Karen references "historical and social contexts," questions individual models of composing, and posits her aim as helping students cultivate a "public voice," which she contrasts with the more individual, naturalized conceptions of voice she had before. Her goals for her students seem to be goals for herself as well; in revisualizing literacy by placing the individual within the context of society, she begins a process of taking on and mastering the discourse of composition studies.

Karen's personal history with the article by Jarratt that she references in her narrative provides some context for her literacy renegotiation. In the article, which the practicum students read for a meeting toward the end of the semester, Jarratt (2003) argues that expressivist discourses do not adequately prepare students, especially women and people of color, for the conflict-based discourse that is part of our society. She especially takes issue with Elbow's (1998) idea of the classroom as a value-free zone. Jarratt (2003) argues, "Despite the efficacy of intuitive responses, I contend that we need more, especially in the area of teacher-training. We need a theory and practice more adequately attuned than expressivism is to the social complexities of our classrooms and the political exigencies of our country" (269). Jarratt's contention (which I agree with) is that, in order to become better teachers, graduate instructors like Karen need access to theories and practices that recognize the social, contextual, and ideological nature of literacy.

To put Karen's response to this idea in context, I briefly divert to that practicum meeting in mid-November. David had divided the class into groups, and Karen was in a group that included two male students, Blake and Anthony, and one other female student, Grace. Anthony was the first to speak, and he went into a diatribe, listing the shortcomings of Jarratt's argument. Karen initially responded in defense of the article, saying "I actually kind of liked it" (field notes, November 19, 2010). However, after Blake commented that "it sets up these feminists in the beginning as straw men," Karen seemed to amend her argument, saying, "It does seem a bit contrived, like it's making something out of nothing."

As I observed the group interacting, I was struck by the irony of it: Karen seemed initially to support Jarratt's argument, but then perhaps felt silenced by the two men in her group. This was the very situation Jarratt argues would happen in a classroom environment that asks students to be too "open" to others' views. As this irony suggests, much of the dissent in the group appeared to be based on a misunderstanding of Jarratt's argument that resulted from their lack of familiarity with the scholarship she was citing and the history of the field within which she was writing.

But in my interview with Karen immediately following that class, I asked her about the views she expressed on Jarratt's article, and her explanation didn't support my conclusion that she had been silenced. She told me, "To be honest with you, I didn't particularly like" Jarratt's article, explaining that Jarrett's views were "too extreme" (pers. comm., November 19, 2010). However, Karen appeared to reconsider Jarratt's article when we placed her argument in the context of her classroom. When we talked about Jarratt's critique of the idea that we should validate all student experience, Karen explained,

> I have a kid right now, he wrote . . . oh, I haven't read his paper yet . . . that will help me, but his paper's about justifying slavery, you know? Because he went from an extreme of not being able to argue anything to going to another extreme and arguing something like, I think he's trying to be original, but it's too far. So I had to talk him about that. . . . I won't validate, I won't say, you can write anything you want.

After Karen said this, I pointed out that it seemed as if she was actually agreeing with Jarratt, who says women and people of color in particular cannot be too "open," especially when it comes to oppressive discourse. Karen responded, "To be honest, the way she [Jarratt] said it, I didn't even relate it to what I said to you. I need to read it again."

Although I could see her coming around to Jarratt's views as we discussed them in the interview, given her initial hesitance to embrace them, I was still surprised to see the quote at the end of Karen's revised narrative, a significant place because it marked the culmination of her semester of learning and literacy development. But while it would be easy to take Karen's narrative of conversion at face value, like Welch (1993), I think we must listen for other truths these narratives reveal. As Karen discloses in her introduction to her narrative, changing her views of literacy seems more crucial because of her decision to identify herself as a scholar in the field of composition and rhetoric. She states, "At this juncture in my teaching career, . . . I am obliged to re-imagine myself as college professor specializing in composition and rhetoric" ("Literacy Narrative Final," 2010). I quote this passage because I think one of the key words in it is "obliged." That is, Karen makes a conscious decision to realign her literacy worldview, even if she is not yet fully aware of the implications. Moreover, in spite of David's openness to differing literacy ideologies, Karen appears to think that changing her worldview is mandatory if she is to truly be a member of the discipline of composition and rhetoric. I discuss Karen's decision further in the conclusion to this chapter because I think it points to the possibility for future change but also to the difficulty of doing so in such a short time frame. That is, even for instructors who embrace the liminal nature of their early experiences with composition pedagogy and begin the process of interrogating their views, becoming a teacher is a long, developmental process.

LILY AND KAREN IN THE CLASSROOM: THE TEACHING OBSERVATIONS

As a scholar and teacher more committed to social and rhetorical understandings of literacy, I had some reservations when I observed practices I associate with literacy for personal growth in the classroom. Yet, perhaps because Lily and Karen viewed literacy as enjoyment, their students often seemed incredibly engaged in their classes. Indeed, witnessing Lily's and Karen's teaching made me let go of some of my misgivings about personal views of literacy as they relate to teaching. Even the graduate instructors who were initially skeptical of personal views of literacy found pedagogies that encouraged students to connect with what they were writing (like starting class off with a journal response connecting the reading to their experience) an easy way in to addressing other literacy goals. This realization is particularly poignant in an era that has again begun to question such strategies as being indulgent and counterproductive.[3] While I end this section by pointing to some of the limitations of pedagogies built only from personal-growth perspectives, I also think Lily's and Karen's successes in the classroom point to the continuing importance of process and expressivist pedagogies in the field of composition.

Lily's Classes: Alignment, Authenticity, and Affirmation
Perhaps because of her background in education and the fact that she was working out her own insecurities about being a

student in a competitive doctoral program, Lily thought it was important to affirm her students' contributions in the classroom and in their papers. The first time I visited her class, her students had just read the first fifty pages of *Kindred* by Butler (2003). After starting the class with a journal response that asked them to respond to a question about the reading, Lily asked, "So what did you think of *Kindred*? Ethan came in and told me the book was boring" (field notes, October 26, 2010).

As students shared their responses, Lily's most frequent response was to emphasize what her students' experiences of reading the novel had in common. As students remarked on their experience of the time travel and other science-fiction elements of the book, Lily repeated at intervals the phrases, "I think a lot of people had that experience" and "I think you're not alone" (field notes, October 26, 2010). Following the teaching observation, Lily told me one of the main goals of her teaching was "promoting student voice" (pers. comm., October 26, 2010). I responded to Lily that at some points, it did appear important to her to "validate" her students' perspectives. Lily replied,

> It's like really important to me to make it safe to talk. . . . They begin talking a lot more once they've realized I wasn't going to embarrass them or whatever. Because I hate . . . when I'm making a comment, as a student, and it gets brushed over.

This exchange was significant in that it showed Lily's commitment to creating a safe space for students within the classroom. For Lily, as for many of the expressivists, voice is a means to empowerment. Her comments back to her students were her way of playing Elbow's (1998) believing game in class.[4] She channeled her energy into imagining herself in her students' positions, trying to see the text as they did.

The above exchange also indicated the possibility that her own desire for affirmation throughout her schooling and from the professors of her graduate seminars influenced her goal of promoting student voice in the class she was teaching. Although Lily didn't mention her Austrian professor here, he was probably one of those professors who had made her feel "brushed over," demonstrating how values and concerns from graduate instructors' past literacy transfer into their teaching. Even more than transferring, though, Lily's prior experiences with literacy seemed determining, even in moments in which she didn't directly acknowledge their influence. When I observed Lily's class the following spring, she repeated the idea (mentioned in her October 15, 2010 interview) of "aligning what you think, feel, do, and say," which is achieved through yoga (field notes, February 21, 2011). This time, her statement came in the context of telling her students that connecting to what they were writing about was another way of achieving this alignment. After having her students write in their journals, one student volunteered, "I think of writing as writing down, like, historical things or facts, and then my argument. But, I guess I need to connect more personally to what I'm writing." Lily responded, saying,

> Yeah, sometimes it's hard when we're writing about a social issue, to connect to it personally. The only way it's going to be interesting to read is if you find a connection to it, and if you think what you say and what you do and what you feel are aligned. If you're doing something you don't love or are bored of, and there's a misalignment, it's not going to work.

Lily's students seemed to be experiencing this "misalignment" because they felt they were just writing to respond to an assignment. In addition, they were required to take a critical stance on a historical example of nonviolence, which required them to examine an event with which they were initially unfamiliar. This led, for the young man I quoted above, to a feeling of just recording "facts." This perception is one of the potential effects of a curriculum that doesn't explicitly create opportunities for students to identify a personal stake in what they are writing, and I think it points to the value of some of Lily's and Karen's approaches to pedagogy.

Karen's Classes: Making It Interesting

Karen channeled her frustration about her past and present school-based assignments into her role as a teacher. She had encountered teachers whose effect was stultifying rather than inspiring, and she became determined not to do the same to her own students. Her solution to what she saw as the disconnection school can create between a student and their natural literacy abilities was to communicate her own passion for literacy. However Karen also expressed concern for how to realize this in practice.

> When I began teaching, I focused on sharing the most effective academic writing formats and techniques so my students could excel scholastically. Now, however, I worry that these formats do not truly allow my students to express all aspects of their lives through the medium of writing. Anne Lamott's *Bird by Bird: Instructions of Writing and Life* and Stephen Kings *On Writing: A Memoir of the Craft* both have influenced me to think, as they do, that my students need to be able to use more than reason to communicate their unique observations. ("Literacy Narrative Draft," 2010)

In this statement, Karen communicates perhaps her most straightforwardly expressivist ideas. For Karen, "formats and techniques" cannot help her students, precluding a pedagogy that includes direct instruction in writing and attention to language. I could see, for example, Karen dismissing a class exercise that compares the structure of a scientific article to the structure of an article in the humanities by describing the scientific article as too focused on format. Karen instead wants language to exist as a medium for expression. Her argument that students need "more than reason" also questions traditional academic argumentation in favor of what she sees as more creative and expressive writing.

Like Lily, Karen emphasized that she wanted to act as a supportive presence for her students in the classroom. And also like Lily, the most defining feature of Karen's pedagogy was her focus on helping students become personally invested in reading and writing. When I came into her class the second time I observed her, she had written on the board, "What makes you become interested in a text/presentation?" (field notes, March 4, 2011). After students had brainstormed a list of attributes, like "creativity/originality" and "humor," Karen had them use this list as a guide to score the groups that were presenting. Then she announced, "Now, what you're going to do with this list is, you're going to do a presentation, and I want those of you not in the group . . . to give the following feedback." She then wrote on the board, "What interested me most?" and "What could have been done to influence me more to become interested?"

Karen helped her students think about making their pieces more interesting and original by giving a workshop on what she called "interest grabbers"—those first few sentences of a piece of writing that should, in Karen's view, grab the attention of the reader, regardless of genre. She told me,

> If you don't start your paper in some way that engages people . . . people aren't going to want to read what you have to say. . . . It's going to become dry and boring, and should academic writing be dry and boring? Well, no. I don't think so, and that's part of my own little personal agenda. (pers. comm., March 4, 2011)

For Karen, as for Lily, making writing interesting involved students investing in it personally and relating it to their lives. Karen's agenda appeared to be a reaction against having to read and write dry academic texts, and she certainly wasn't alone in her critiques of academic writing.

However, I would be remiss if I didn't also point to some of the problems with Karen's and Lily's assumptions, not in order to blame them for having these views but rather to think through ways practica instructors can create occasions for graduate instructors to consider their implications. As a literacy theorist, I see literacy as more expansive than just academic writing. However, I was troubled that Karen never made the move from journalistic texts to academic ones. I felt a similar moment of concern when I visited Lily's class the second time and she was giving her students "a poetry day" as a sort of respite before they had to turn in their first draft of the second paper (field notes, February 21, 2011). Karen's and Lily's activities showed a recognition that academic writing is much less narrow and contained than we think it is, and that engaging students in what interests them and allowing them to bring in their lives outside school can well be productive teaching strategies.

And yet, I could also see Karen's activity on interest grabbers as possibly more relevant for students in a composition classroom if she had brought in academic essays as well, perhaps from a variety of different fields, and had students examine those to determine whether the same rules applied. Students could even have come upon the realization that what is interesting in one context and for a certain audience might not be interesting for others, recognizing the role of genre in writing. That is, Karen's conception of what is "interesting" assumes a universal understanding of audience derived from a decontextualized view of literacy. Moreover, Karen's mandate that students "make up an original argument," which she further clarified as "try[ing not] to write the same thing" as their classmates, is also inherently difficult for students (field notes, March 4, 2011). How, one wonders, is a student supposed to know what every other student has decided to write about so they can make their own papers different and original? How is any student not familiar with the discourse community within which they are writing supposed to know what constitutes a new idea within that community?

Nevertheless, I do see these activities as having value, and I think, if I were the practicum instructor, my critiques of Karen's activity on interest grabbers and Lily's poetry day could be framed in ways that honor the experiences and knowledge they bring while also making them aware of other ways to approach these workshops to connect them to other genres of writing.

Lily also conceived of good writing as something that demanded personal investment that couldn't really be taught. She stated,

> I've been telling all of them that, like, this isn't something that I can teach you, to care about your papers and be interested in your papers, but that's what makes good writing, is when you're personally invested in what you're writing about. And so the way to do that is . . . using writing as a way to talk about your personal self, yourself as a person and then translate that . . . into an academic language. (pers. comm., February 21, 2011)

Lily's description of engagement as energy is, I think, particularly apt. However, my goal as a practica instructor would be to steer her towards reenvisioning teaching as more than mechanical instruction that gets in the way of students' natural interests and capabilities. That is, Lily needs to conceptualize "teaching" itself more broadly so it can include both explicit instruction in writing and also creating occasions when students can, in fact, become personally invested in their writing.

CONCLUSION: BEYOND THE GARRET MODEL OF LITERACY

My attitude towards Karen's and Lily's views of writing and teaching was similar to some of the reservations expressed in the literature on graduate-instructor education I describe at the beginning of this chapter. Much like Rankin (1994) and Bishop (1990), I saw Karen and Lily's views as outdated. And, like Ebest (2005), I had concerns that Karen and Lily would "continue to pass on the misperception that composing is a private, individual process not to be interfered with for fear of quashing creativity" (57). In *A Teaching Subject*, Joseph Harris (1997) criticizes theorists who make "voice" a determinant of good writing and argues that if we see writing in this way, it becomes unteachable. Harris contends, "The rhetoric of authenticity . . . sets up a situation where a certain kind of talk or teaching becomes next to impossible. For if what counts is less what a writer has to say than how much he really means or feels it, then the measure of good writing becomes its genuineness or sincerity. And how do you tell *that?*" (32)

Lily's comment "this isn't something that I can teach you, to care about your papers" hit on a similar concern (pers. comm., February 21, 2011). Nevertheless, Lily did seem to be identifying ways she could help students find a personal investment in what they were writing by creating situations in which they could transform texts into something meaningful by writing themselves in.

To put it another way, visiting Karen's and Lily's classrooms also *changed me*. Karen's use of journalistic texts and Lily's use of poetry constituted a broadening of FYC beyond academic texts, which may be a good thing in that both Karen and Lily were finding ways to engage their students through a wide range of genres and literacy practices and were drawing on their own interests and experiences with literacy do to this. Although I still maintain that one of the goals of practica instructors should be to help students like Karen and Lily make explicit connections to academic writing so their students perceive activities like the ones Karen and Lily designed as relevant to the rest of their academic work (and to integrate concepts like having a personal voice into more contingent, situated understandings of identity), I cannot imagine shoehorning either Karen or Lily into a narrowly academic curriculum so that I become yet another authoritarian teacher (or in this case, authoritarian mentor/researcher). Moreover, as Goldblatt (2017) recently argued in his defense of expressivism in *CCC*, composition's recent focus on academic writing over "the experience of writing," something that was important and meaningful for both Lily and Karen, risks preventing new graduate instructors from discovering how their experiences might translate into meaningful pedagogy and connections with their students (461).

Despite the fact that she had more experience in the classroom, Karen appeared more willing to reconsider her conception of literacy than was Lily. Karen used her final literacy narrative as an opportunity to reconsider her views of literacy, as well as a space for overcoming some of the flattened ways she was seeing the undergraduates in her course experience literacy. During our interview, I asked Karen whether her experiences of not having much choice in what she was writing about for one of her graduate seminars made her sympathize with her students. However, she initially effaced this connection (see Dryer 2012). Karen told me she thought her undergraduates could simply go to their professors and "propose different paper topics" (pers. comm., November 19, 2010). However, she saw her own situation as allowing for less personal choice and self-exploration than her students had. In her final narrative, she reconsiders this initial position, stating,

> When Meaghan interviewed me, she asked me if this experience [of writing papers for the Introduction to Graduate Study seminar] made me empathetic toward my students' struggles to

master academic writing. Initially, I said no, but I was wrong. It has and it should because keeping this in mind will make me have more patience when my students become overwhelmed by the writing expectations of the academy. ("Literacy Narrative Final," 2010)

Karen recognizes, in this statement, that both she and her students are negotiating the often complex and prescriptive writing expectations of the academy. Her realization probably happened in part because of her identification of teaching as a scholarly practice, an identification we should encourage for other graduate instructors as well. In addition, in choosing composition and rhetoric as her field of study, she made the connection between teaching and scholarship more relevant, as she saw it as impacting her future as a successful scholar. In other words, Karen's insights were motivated by a conscious decision about what she wanted her identity as a teacher and scholar to be. This challenges assumptions about how values surrounding literacy become sedimented in more experienced teachers and further suggests that the *stance* experienced teachers take towards their learning may overcome what they "know" based on their experiences.

Karen's reconsideration seems prompted by what Yancey, Robertson, and Taczak (2014) refer to as a "critical incident," which they define as "a failed effort to address a new task that prompts critical ways of thinking about what writing is and how to do it" (104). The critical incident Karen refers to is her experience of not doing well on her paper in her Introduction to Graduate Study class, which forced her to rethink how to write a paper. Further, the occasion of our interview prompted Karen to see parallels between her experience and her students,' demonstrating how the interview acted as an intervention in her ways of thinking about literacy. As in the experiences of the graduate instructors discussed in Berkenkotter, Huckin, and Ackerman (1988) and Estrem and Reid (2012), Karen's insight is the result of her opportunity to reflect on her experiences with the aid of someone knowledgeable in composition theory and pedagogy. This outcome demonstrates that mentoring experiences outside the formal space of the practicum can have a significant impact on graduate instructors as they come to terms with the conflicts that arise among their personal beliefs, their discipline, and the demands and challenges of teaching composition.

Karen would reconsider other ideas in her final narrative as well, where she explicitly begins to integrate more social understandings of literacy into her narrative, using concepts from Bartholomae's "Inventing the University" (1985) to understand how she is beginning to take on new ways of knowing as a response to the expectations of her seminar teachers. However, Karen's narrative still contains ideas associated with literacy for personal growth, embodied in her references to literacy as "visual conception, the voices and guidance of women and outsiders, stoking my stuttering inventive flame and introspection" ("Literacy Narrative Final," 2010). Although Karen switches from "voice" to "voices," her placement of "introspection" at the end of her description still communicates an individual understanding of literacy. To put it another way, Karen's experience in the practicum cannot be simply characterized by either change or no change; she *both changes and stays the same.* Her journey shows reconsiderations are possible in the short period of a semester. However, still present are her original ideas of literacy as a personal journey. At least at this stage in her development, new learning (even though it *is* learning) does not necessarily trump ideas that up until now have been part of her literacy identity.

On the surface, Lily's trajectory could be read more as a story of resistance than Karen's, as she did not appear as willing to reconsider previous ways of thinking about literacy in her final literacy narrative. Even when she does draw on social and contextual conceptions of literacy, she cites her previous graduate program in English education, rather than the practicum, as their source. Yet, Lily's story also challenges narratives of resistance in research on graduate-instructor education. The term *resistance* calls up images of stubbornness and outward (and even disruptive) rebellion. But Lily never outwardly rebelled against readings and often, in practicum meetings, appeared to consider the ideas presented in the readings without voicing objections to them. For Lily, as in the instructors described by Reid, Estrem, and Belcheir (2012), "resistance" is more "inertial" (55). Moreover, in the conclusion to this book, I describe a longer trajectory with which to consider Lily's learning, one that complicates models for learning that indicate new learning completely replaces old.

Although Karen's experience points to the potential for the practicum to play a role in helping graduate instructors reconsider old ways of thinking, taken together, Karen's and Lily's experiences demonstrate its effects may not be realized during the truncated period of a graduate instructor's first semester. Their experiences speak to my overall argument that other sponsors and "systems," such as their previous experiences with teachers, prior graduate education, parents, and even Lily's background in yoga transfer more readily into their conceptions of literacy and their pedagogy (Dryer 2012, 443). To paraphrase Linda Brodkey (1996), the garret scene of writing seems to be what many individuals in US society learn first (59). Yet there are ways to work within these tensions between what new graduate instructors value and the pedagogies we would like to nudge them towards.

WPAs can better support graduate instructors like Lily and Karen by affirming the personal and expressivist roots of our discipline. Many of the texts the graduate instructors were reading for the practicum were what I would describe as *social* and *rhetorical* in nature, yet they either directly responded to or contained subtle traces of prior paradigms that viewed literacy from a much more individual perspective. Bartholomae (1985) spends much of his "Inventing the University" responding to (and arguing against) Linda Flower and John Hayes's (1981) cognitivist framework for understanding the writing process. Jarratt (2003) challenges Sally Miller Gearhart's (1979) stance towards teaching that seeks to minimize conflict and "replace an authoritarian model of education with a nurturing atmosphere," also taking on Elbow's (1998) conflict and value-free description of the writing classroom (265, 267). During the practicum meeting after the graduate instructors had read Jarratt's article, Lily stated that reading it "would have been more valuable if we could have [also] read some of the authors Jarratt mentions, like maybe Elbow and Gearhart" (field notes, November 19, 2010).

I think Lily is right. Whether we are challenging or reaffirming individual models for composing, we must acknowledge the broad influence they have had on the field of composition. Moreover, as Goldblatt (2017) asserts, we should also think more carefully about how much our response to some aspects of the expressivist tradition is motivated by "fear of sounding sentimental or overly mortgaged to the less prestigious aspects of the profession" (457), as well as our association of personal models of composing with women's work. We can also expose graduate instructors to other texts that link expressivism with "social and liberatory" literacy practices and encourage graduate students to use the lenses of critical race and queer theory to critique early expressivism (Burnham and Powell 2013, 113). By presenting texts like Bartholomae's or Jarratt's without a sense of what they are responding to, we risk not engaging with the beliefs of graduate instructors like Karen and Lily, a real danger if we want to better support them as teachers and learners.

3

TEXTS, HIERARCHY, AND RITUAL
Cultural Literacy

It may seem odd to suggest, at a time when "process, not product" was at its height, that our field was text-centric. But it was—thoroughly. Partly, this had to do with the practical demands of teaching writing: assigning, responding, assessing. But it also had to do, no doubt, with the literary and linguistics training of so many comp/rhet people at the time. In any case, composition and rhetoric concerned itself with texts and the making of texts. Literacy was treated as text making (writing) or text taking (reading).

—Deborah Brandt

In the above epigraph from a recent symposium on literacy in *CCC*, Deborah Brandt (2018) describes the effect Shirley Brice Heath's *Ways with Words* had on the field of composition studies. Although Brandt locates these views within composition's history, her description of a "text-centric" literacy conception could well be applied to the current assumptions of many of those working across English studies who, consciously or not, see literacy largely as reading or writing. Brandt's reference to the training of "many comp/rhet people at the time" is a nod to the fact that many of the scholars who were part of the process movement had backgrounds in literary studies, a field that has, for the most part, valued and elevated the text part of the literacy experience.

Following Knoblauch (1990) and Goggin (2008), I term the conception of literacy I examine in this chapter *cultural literacy*. However, in some ways, "text-centric" literacy would be a more suitable descriptor for what are understandings of literacy that

DOI: 10.7330/9781607329343.c003

place texts (and in particular, textual analysis and appreciation) at the center of the literacy experience. Although cultural literacy is often associated with E. D. Hirsch (1988), the graduate instructors I discuss here saw literacy in some markedly different ways from Hirsch's envisioning of literacy as the shared knowledge of a body of texts and ideas that enables readers to comprehend texts because they get most of the intertextual references. The graduate instructors were for the most part uncomfortable with the idea that everyone needs to know a particular body of knowledge. Instead, they often invoked hierarchical views of literacy that elevated individuals because of their knowledge of texts. In other words, these graduate instructors saw themselves as being *truly* literate because of their ability to master difficult, often theoretical, texts.

Cultural-literacy assumptions have had a lasting impact on the broad field of English studies in large part because of literary studies' devotion to "close reading" of (mostly) literary texts (Carillo 2015; Elbow 2002). Because many new graduate instructors have spent a great deal of time studying literature and learning close reading, they feel more comfortable with devoting class time to reading than with teaching writing.[1] However, the graduate instructors I discuss in this chapter also struggled with whether or not this focus was appropriate in a composition classroom. That is, while they attributed great value to the close study of texts, both literary and nonliterary, they wondered whether and how these practices would help their students become better writers.

This text-centric view of literacy was most true of the three literature PhD students, Blake, Garrett, and Jordi. Although Garrett's and Jordi's ideas about literacy were also informed by social/critical understandings, cultural-literacy views were more influential on their teaching and impacted how they processed the pedagogy presented in the practicum. As Garrett said, in describing why he chose to go to graduate school, "I really liked books, I guess" (pers. comm., October 20, 2010). Blake argues similarly in his final literacy narrative that "the literacy I learned at an early age was not through writing or grammar instruction, but through extensive reading" ("Literacy Narrative Draft," 2010). These statements are a reminder that a love of reading and literature, rather than a love of teaching or writing, is often at the heart of why people decide to pursue a graduate degree in English. Although all three of these participants expressed interest in what they were learning in the practicum and wanted to grow as teachers, their belief that knowledge of and appreciation of texts should be their end goal for their students influenced them to choose pedagogical approaches highlighting reading over writing and, moreover, to favor a certain kind of reading practice (New Critical close reading) because it fit with their own past experiences in literature classes.

DEFINING CULTURAL LITERACY

Goggin (2008) defines cultural literacy as literacy "pertaining to the cultured, intellectual person of letters" (53). Although this conception is often associated with canonical literature, for the graduate instructors described in this chapter, the values associated with canonization and the "supposedly stable and timeless" values inscribed in these texts are perhaps more characteristic of Blake's, Garrett's, and Jordi's views, as they often referenced noncanonical texts but still positioned them above other, more transient, topical, or popular works (Knoblauch 1990, 77). Goggin (2008) and Knoblauch (1990) both remark on the conservatism of cultural literacy, especially in contrast to the more "liberal" literacy for personal growth and social/critical literacy; cultural literacy, according to Goggin (2008), reflects composition's role in gatekeeping (80). In other words, knowledge of certain texts, and the theories and historical information associated with them, marks the literate individual as a member of a private club.

Although many of the ideas I label as *cultural literacy* are inculcated in extracurricular sites, a number of them can be traced to understandings of literacy that developed as departments of English came into being at the end of the nineteenth century. As scholars like Susan Miller (1991), Sharon Crowley (1998), and Thomas Miller (2011) have argued, the creation of the first composition and literature courses created a symbiotic but hierarchical relationship between the two disciplines. Although both were positioned as more "relevant" than the defunct classics, literature occupied the higher, more serious and scholarly position in the symbolic system, while composition's status was demeaned and stigmatized (Miller 1991, 51).

This relationship between composition and literature helps explain how literature and the literary canon were able to, in comparison to popular works and "deficient" student texts, achieve their elevated status. After colleges developed the first composition courses, literature could be defined as elevated against the texts produced by students in FYC. Although the study of literature taught students to appreciate great works of literature, for the most part, students were taught to be consumers of texts rather than creators of them (Miller 2011, 118). In other words, composition students were "thought of as 'merely writing,'" not engaging in the "privileged creation" known as "authorship" (Miller 1991, 64).

As with the other conceptions, this literacy view offers both affordances and limitations. In some ways, Jordi, Garrett, and Blake had realistic views of academia and English departments as privileging text-centric literacy beliefs and practices. Yet I suspect many practica instructors and WPAs would want to intervene in such belief systems for a few reasons. First, to return to Brandt's (2018) discussion of Heath's *Ways with Words*, composition scholars have been acculturated to a view of literacy that sees texts as only one aspect of the literacy experience; the influence of literacy studies on composition shifted our focus from texts in isolation to *literacy practices* and *literacy events*, which, as Brandt (2018) argues, got us "out of the box" so we could attune to "the flow of . . . [literacy practices] within larger, patterned social activities" (505). Literacy studies scholars posit that meaning making is going on all the time, not just during times we would immediately recognize as reading or writing.

Second, cultural-literacy views, which see texts and people in terms of hierarchy may, as Grutsch McKinney and Chiseri-Strater (2003) put it, "tread heavily" on practica instructors' "professional identities" because they remind us of the views marginalizing composition we have read about in histories like Miller's (1991) or even the ongoing experiences we have with colleagues in literary studies within our own departments (64).[2] That is, many of the values associated with cultural literacy are in opposition to the work of compositionists, who view literacy as a social practice and who do not privilege canonical texts over the ones produced by students.

Although none of the participants in this study were aware of the development of college English, they all had a tacit sense of the culturally engrained hierarchy of people and texts described by Miller (1991). Yet, it would be a mistake to hold these newcomers accountable for their implicit views or to project our frustration about the marginalization of composition onto them. At different points in the study, Garrett, Jordi, and Blake all acknowledged that textual interpretation by itself is not the goal of the first-year course and began to question views that, once they thought through them, marginalized either their students or the people they cared about. In addition, they had never taught a composition course before, had not, with the exception of Blake, taken a composition course as undergraduates, and were unfamiliar with composition theory. Thus, while I take a critical view of some of the assumptions and practices I describe in this chapter, I also argue that the onus is on us, as WPAs, as well as more broadly on English departments who are educating and professionalizing graduate students, to help them arrive at broader, more inclusive understandings of literacy. Indeed, at many points in their narratives and interviews, Garrett, Jordi, and Blake showed evidence that they were beginning to question what they realized were exclusionary beliefs about literacy.

CULTURAL LITERACY AND GRADUATE-INSTRUCTOR CONCEPTIONS

Of the codes for conceptions of literacy, I assigned cultural literacy 246 times, the third highest frequency behind literacy for

Table 3.1. Numbers for cultural literacy, as a ratio and a percentage of each focal participant's total codes

Participant	Discipline	Ratio of cultural-literacy codes to participant's total codes	Percentage of cultural-literacy codes
Blake	literature	76/111	68.5
Garrett	literature	42/104	40.4
Jordi	literature	67/167	40.1
Max	creative writing	23/104	22.1
Karen	comp/rhet	8/101	7.9
Barbara	creative writing	11/143	7.7
Lily	comp/rhet	13/210	6.2

personal growth (n=355) and social/critical literacy (n= 274). While it didn't appear as frequently as literacy for personal growth, cultural literacy showed up almost as much as social/ critical literacy. As table 3.1 below indicates, text and literature-centric notions of literacy were pervasive among a particular subset of the participants: the PhD students in literature.

In table 3.1, I rank the seven focal participants according to the percentage the code for cultural literacy represents in the total number of codes for conceptions of literacy.

None of the participants in this study advocated a national curriculum or required reading lists, as Hirsch (1988) does. In fact, when I had them rank writing assignments during the Assignment-Ranking Activity (see appendix C), they reacted negatively to the idea that every American should have knowledge of a set of culturally sanctioned works, labeling this idea as "elitist" and "offensive." During the activity, four students in the practicum (none of whom were focal participants) crossed out the phrase "knowledge of which all literate Americans should have," which I paraphrased from the subtitle to Hirsch's (1988) *Cultural Literacy*. This response was unique in that no one crossed out any portion of any of the other assignments in the activity.

Mentions of cultural literacy doubled from the initial drafts of the literacy narratives the seven focal participants wrote to the revised narratives turned in at the end of the semester, going from twenty-five content units for cultural literacy in the early drafts to fifty. However, the content units overall more than doubled from the first to the second set of literacy narratives.[3] Thus, this doubling seems to indicate that the ideas expressed in the early ones were developed and explored in the final narratives. Perhaps most significant, though, the changes between the narratives suggest the social/critical emphasis in the practicum did not deter the graduate instructors from text-centric views. However, the graduate instructors were more conscious and critical of them, at times vacillating between views they had once not questioned and more self-aware, reflexive views of their literacy.

In the remainder of this chapter, I discuss data from Garrett's, Jordi's, and Blake's interviews and literacy narratives to develop more complete pictures of how each saw literacy. To begin, I characterize the literacy experiences that informed Jordi's and Garrett's conceptions of literacy, focusing specifically on the idea of ritual or initiation. Whereas both Garrett and Jordi viewed literacy as a transformative "state of grace," their views of literacy were largely secularized (see Scribner 1984). Blake's, on the other hand, appeared directly connected to his upbringing in a conservative Protestant home. In foregrounding the religious and ritualistic aspects of their literacy experiences, I draw attention to how deeply engrained and meaningful these text-centric conceptions were for Jordi, Garrett, and Blake. By this I mean if one perceives oneself as being inducted into a special literacy club, it becomes difficult to shake the sense of literacy as hierarchical.

Although the narrative arcs of these three's literacy stories are similar in that all share a deep devotion to texts and interpretation and are structured as stories of initiation, Jordi, Garrett and Blake came from very different backgrounds. Jordi identified as an academia brat; her father was an English professor, her mother was an English teacher, and her stepfather was a psychology professor, making her upbringing the most overtly academic. Garrett grew up in a working-class family in the Midwest in which college was neither guaranteed nor even expected. Because he couldn't afford college right after high school, he initially joined the National Guard. Finally, Blake grew up in a conservative Presbyterian family in the Northeast, was homeschooled until he was in college, and held some conservative political views (like being pro-life).

Perhaps related to the hierarchical nature of cultural literacy, I should note some limitations with the case studies I present in this chapter. As in the last chapter, all the participants I describe here are white and (except for Garrett) middle class. Indeed, in the moments when Garrett discussed his working-class background, he also appeared more apt to see and challenge the hierarchical nature of this literacy conception. These participants also made some ableist assumptions about their students, which could be related to the hierarchies described earlier. I thus end this chapter by considering how insights from disability studies could help them reexamine their literacy conceptions.

Jordi's Initiation into Academia

Jordi's narrative of her initiation into the academy, which details her completion of her undergraduate senior thesis on T. S. Eliot, tells the story of her joining her English-professor father's profession, even though her narrative resists that idea that he influenced her. In her first literacy narrative, she acknowledges but also downplays his influence, stating that her honors-thesis advisor was also her father's dissertation advisor, that she had had dinner at his house, and that she was partially named after his daughter ("Literacy Narrative Draft," 2010). Despite her father's undeniable involvement in and influence on her entrance into academia, Jordi proclaims at the end of the first paragraph of her first literacy narrative, "My thesis experience is the reason I am who I am today: an English grad student." Her willingness to ascribe her identity to a text, her thesis, rather than to a person, her father, is evidence of the extent to which text-centric understandings of literacy had shaped her beliefs.

Her narrative calls attention to the centrality of texts in her life but obscures how the presence of those texts was only one aspect of her family's literacy practices.

Jordi describes her pre-thesis self as "clueless" and "blissful[ly] ignorant," highlighting the ignorance of the novice or preinitiate into the academic elite and signaling that this is to be a story of initiation ("Literacy Narrative Draft," 2010). She recounts the experience of defending her thesis, saying,

> I was sweating nervously by the time I entered the conference room, uncomfortable in heels and business attire at one end of the long table, with my three interrogators looking at me expectantly from the other end. But I nailed it. I had spent a whole year on this, and I knew my stuff. . . . I still remember the last question, from my out-of-department committee member. . . . "Do you think anyone has done something like this before?" he asked. . . . I saw the glint of what I now know to be a huge compliment: I had done something innovative in a well-established field.

With this claiming of her own intellectual property, Jordi marks herself as an initiate into the ivory tower. That this process is ensconced in ceremony, with the defense and its "three interrogators" acting as an initiation ritual, underscores the similarity between these academic procedures and religious ceremonies, which often mark a crossing over from one state to the other: from single to married, from sinner to saved. Jordi portrays her initiation as a trial by fire, but one in which she was ultimately victorious and could therefore take her place among the literate.

Jordi ends the narrative by contrasting her defense with what she did afterwards. She says, "I went back to my dorm and watched *Oprah*. I'm not sure if this is more significant because I had hardly watched TV in the past year or because it completely counters all things academic, which I had just defended in the hour before" ("Literacy Narrative Draft," 2010). The contrast of academia with pop culture further underscores Jordi's understanding of what she has done as something reserved for the academic elite, set apart from popular culture and mass consumption.

In her revised narrative, Jordi spends more time thinking about how people (rather than texts) have acted as literacy sponsors and informed her values and beliefs about literacy. Much like Karen (discussed in the last chapter), she consciously allies her views more closely with ones communicated in the practicum; she uses the term "literacy" throughout instead of "reading and writing," asserts that it is "fundamentally social," and cites an article from the practicum by Mariolina Salvatori ("Literacy Narrative Draft," 2010). In many ways, this narrative reflects that Jordi is a good student; she is receptive and organized, always questioning and refining her teaching approaches. However, she also struggles to see student writing as similar to the literature she is used to analyzing. Although she uses the practicum as a space for self-reflection and questioning her preconceptions, her experiences also show that values cemented in ritual can be difficult to shake, especially in a hectic first semester of teaching. In other words, although her literacy narrative could be read as demonstrating the success of the practicum's pedagogy, the seeds the practicum planted in her thinking about literacy would require more time and continued support in order to change her thinking about literacy in more fundamental ways.

Garrett's Fall from Grace

As described in his first narrative, Garrett's initiation took place not as part of an academic ritual but in his realization of the hierarchy the academic elite impose upon texts. Garrett begins by describing reading with his grandmother, saying,

> She is the first person I remember sharing an enjoyment for reading with. Because my parents worked crazy hours at their jobs and . . . did not have money for childcare, I spent a good deal of time at my grandparents' house growing up. One of my earliest memories reading with her is looking at a picture of Tom and Becky stuck in that cave in Hannibal. I can still see the downward angle of the picture. . . . Figures of the bats partially emerge into the frame and Tom and Becky stand below shivering. ("Literacy Narrative Draft" 2010)

A great deal of Garrett's narrative is about his grandmother. Nevertheless, central to this experience is the text; Garrett recalls not the tone his grandmother's voice takes when she reads or the way she looked but the images in this book. However, Garrett began to view his grandmother's reading habits, which he describes as "tend[ing] toward detective fiction" and "David Baldacci" in a different light ("Literacy Narrative Draft," 2010). At the time of the incident that marked Garrett's passage into the metaphorical "literary club," he was in the second grade and the "book of the moment was *Scary Stories to Tell in the Dark* by Alvin Schwartz." Garrett describes the book and his desire to obtain it, saying that as soon as the librarian "released" his class to pick out their books, "there was a mad stampede to this Schwartz book." He describes coming to a realization of the hierarchy of texts on one of these library days, recalling,

> When I was racing with the others to grab that Schwartz book, Quinn went and got himself recognized as a good reader. One day I noticed that he was on the other side of the room, browsing in the damned adult section—a fact Ms. Moretz was later happy to announce to the entire class, suggesting that the rest of the class (including myself) might endeavor to become better readers, like Quinn. . . . Before this incident, I cannot remember ever being self-conscious about how I read, or what I read, or what others were reading.

Garrett's narrative contains significant parallels to Brodkey's (1996) description of the first time she entered the adult section of her own public library, which she describes as "literally read[ing] my way out of the children's library" (34). Garrett witnessed someone *else* accomplishing this feat and felt the attendant shame that it wasn't him. In this moment the "Schwartz book" went from desired object to something repellent—an object for consumption not unlike *Oprah* in Jordi's literacy narrative. Garrett thus portrays himself as someone intimately concerned with "quality," which he posits in opposition to popular works. In his fall from innocence, he became ashamed. Reading suddenly became more than just a harmless, leisure activity; it was now symbolic of a literary elite.

Garrett's new, more refined taste served as a standard, the lens through which he viewed the world after he became aware of the hierarchy of texts. He concludes his first narrative, saying,

> Since then, I have felt caught between my consciousness of what is defined as *good* reading and writing. I am continually trapped between my desire to equal my projection of the Quinns of the world and my desire to not establish that hierarchy. Though I try not to judge my grandmother for reading detective fiction, I do. Of course, she sits on some imaginary level above people who do not care to read at all but this imaginary level is still an ethical failure on her part. The irony, of course, is that my grandmother taught me to like reading and Quinn taught me to fear it. ("Literacy Narrative Draft," 2010)

Garrett's heart-wrenching realization is, I suspect, something many people in the fields comprising English studies (including composition) would recognize: books are not mere play.

I don't think Garrett tells this story in order to marginalize his grandmother, a woman who took care of him in his parents' absence and who was (until Quinn) his most important literacy sponsor. Instead, he recognizes there is something unfair about his judgment of her, and I think he includes this story in order to work through it and see if there is a way of viewing literacy that doesn't place his grandmother below him in a literary hierarchy. His description of reading as an activity to be feared says something about what a concentration on canonical or "quality" texts can do, both to us and to the students we teach. Although I am sure many professors in literary studies teach lessons and even entire courses with the purpose of challenging canonical understandings of literacy, somehow this isn't the message many graduate students hear. Indeed, for students like Garrett, English departments probably contain competing, often contradictory messages about literacy. Even if students like Garrett aren't hearing views from professors that state the superiority of British over American literature, of literary criticism over scientific writing, or of teaching literature courses over teaching composition (all sentiments I heard during my own graduate-school experience), many of the *practices* associated with graduate school, which is itself exclusionary and highly steeped in ritual, may end up reinforcing cultural commonplaces that depict the study of English as learning "the classics." Indeed, graduate programs themselves may be inherently conservative in their emphasis on past knowledge and practices, even in the discovery of the new. Notably, the same could be said of composition studies, which now has its own "canon" of research and genealogy of researchers.

Garrett reframes his revised narrative into a story of loss and violence. For him, "the pre-lapsarian" view of literacy is the one, represented by his grandmother, in which he could simply enjoy reading. In the "post-lapsarian view," literacy becomes something violent to be feared. He describes "post-lapsarian" literacy as something "that has historically been used by individuals and groups to enslave others" ("Literacy Narrative Final," 2010), an observation similar to Elspeth Stuckey's (1991) understanding of literacy as violence, which argues that literacy educators must acknowledge literacy's role in maintaining hegemony (see also Graff 2001). Garrett's revised narrative is thus a sophisticated take on literacy's double-edged sword. In the face of his realizations about literacy, Garrett is hopeful but realistic, trying to envision how he, as an educator, could mitigate literacy's violence.

But the most prescient moment Garrett added to his later narrative had to do with his friend Quinn. After high school, Quinn got to attend college while Garrett, who couldn't afford it, joined the Army National Guard. He describes visiting Quinn in college, where Quinn disparaged him for liking Pink Floyd's "Wish You Were Here" ("Literacy Narrative Final," 2010). Much as Quinn had disillusioned Garrett of his liking of the *Scary Stories* book, during that visit he disenchanted Garrett of his fondness for the Pink Floyd song. Garrett explains,

> In my mind, I have set him up as an ideal arbiter of taste, not only in terms of what one should like but also what one should *be* like. The Quinn in my head is not a real person; he is a static thing that does not change, make mistakes, or even operate by any principles that could be spoken aloud. ("Literacy Narrative Final," 2010)

Here, Garrett articulates literacy in the vein of Arnoldian humanism in which what a person likes (their taste) determines the quality of their character and educational achievement. Likewise, he feels disgraced when he chooses the "wrong" side in intellectual matters. But as in his earlier narrative, Garrett struggles to combat these views in light of more critical understandings of literacy presented in the practicum, recognizing he must get beyond the Quinns of the world if he wants to move toward ways of understanding literacy that will be more productive for him in his teaching. He ends his revised narrative saying, "I know that building culture, that which is formed from the work of people, is what I cherish most." In moving towards this more progressive view of culture as something evolving and forward looking rather than static and backward looking, Garrett indicates the necessity of evolving beyond his former understanding of literacy. As someone who came from a working-class background and who couldn't immediately afford college, he recognizes and resists the class-based, hierarchical views of literacy as limiting, even as they are simultaneously challenged and reinforced in his graduate-school curriculum. Taken together, Garrett's narratives demonstrate the need for new graduate instructors to both acknowledge these past views and begin a process of opening them up and resituating them. For Garrett, canonical, text-centric views are compelling, but he seems equally motivated to explore how literacy can be more.

Blake: Religion and "Obsessive" Reading

The participant whose conception of literacy seemed most influenced by cultural literacy was Blake, who, unlike Jordi and Garrett, did not seem swayed by a competing facet of his literacy conception. In fact, I came to see Blake (68.5 percent for cultural literacy) and Lily (69.0 percent for literacy for personal growth) as having the most relatively "pure" conceptions of literacy of the seven focal participants. These two also *appeared* the least changed by their experience in the practicum.

A first-year PhD student in literature, twenty-three-year-old Blake gave off a mixture of confidence and trepidation. I first began to think about Blake's conception of literacy during a conversation in the practicum after the graduate instructors had collected their first batch of student papers. Responding to a journal prompt in the practicum that asked the graduate instructors to reflect on their conception of teaching before they began teaching compared to what is was currently, Blake said to the rest of the class,

> I've found that their actual writing, the grammar and so forth, isn't really the issue. Most of them have a decent grasp on that. But I'm a bit concerned with their souls. They make their arguments solely on pragmatic grounds. None of them are using ethical arguments. (field notes, September 24, 2010)

Blake made this comment, and others like it, with such confidence and bravado that I came to look forward to what he would say in the course. His intelligence made him a favorite among his seminar teachers and someone whose views were often discussed among the other graduate instructors. As in Garrett's stories about Quinn, I got a strong sense from Blake that he had internalized a set of standards that served to differentiate levels of texts and literacy. In addition, Blake, like Jordi, seemed to value the culture of academia and the kind of work academics do.

Blake had been home schooled for his entire elementary- and secondary-school education. In our interview, he described typing up his own transcript when he applied to college, which the president of the home-schooling board, who was also the minister of his church, signed. When I asked Blake about why his parents chose to homeschool him, he replied,

> I think partly it was a religious thing. . . . I come from a pretty strict, conservative Presbyterian background. They were concerned about things like, I don't know, sex ed and evolution and things like that. And then, I think they just figured they could probably do a better job, which is very much my reasoning. My wife and I are planning on homeschooling our son. (pers. comm., November 1, 2010)

This conservative religious background also connected, for Blake, with a kind of conservatism with regards to literacy. Although Blake acknowledged his students were coming from different backgrounds, he was influenced by an upbringing that inculcated not just an appreciation of but also a reverence for texts.

In his revised literacy narrative, Blake describes the impact his religious background had on his conception of literacy. He explains,

> The two dominant aspects—indeed, the two governing paradigms—of life under my parent's roof were homeschooling and Protestant Christianity. . . . One very consistent rule in my parents' house was that first thing in the morning, "required reading" had to be completed. Required reading usually consisted of three books: the Bible, a work of nonfiction (usually either history or natural science) and a work of fiction. This last would be selected by my mother with an eye toward challenging us. Sometimes she overshot the mark; I have no idea what *Treasure Island* was about. I read it anyway, conscientiously passing my eyes over each word in succession. When I had finished a chapter from each book, I was allowed to leave my room. A considerable portion of the remainder of the morning would be taken up in further reading, not by us, but by my mother, who spent an hour or two each morning reading aloud. ("Literacy Narrative Final," 2010)

Blake conveys a sense of ceremoniousness and duty to the sacred object of the text in his description of passing his "eyes over each word in succession," even if this doesn't result in comprehension. Although the sense of literacy as salvation is also pervasive in Jordi's and Garrett's descriptions, it is often secularized or treated as symbolic. In Blake's descriptions, however, this religious understanding of texts is much more overt. Given how Blake describes being held captive in his room, as well as the fact that his mother also read aloud to him for two hours a day, the sheer volume of texts he must have consumed is immense.

Blake's characterization of his literacy experiences in terms of obligation and conscientiousness is also present in his September 2, 2010, Blackboard post, in which he says,

I said I was a conscientious reader. Actually, I was an obsessive reader. The idea of skipping a reading assignment was something I could barely wrap my mind around. Even when I didn't understand a word, I would dutifully pass my eyes over every single line until I came to the end.

Blake conveys how much his upbringing has inculcated in him a sense of duty and perhaps also fear when it comes to reading the texts his mother and later his college professors assigned him. That is, even as an adult, he is influenced by those mornings when he could not leave his room until he finished his reading, and he takes the same approach in college and then graduate school, where his child's sense of wanting to live up to parental expectations translates to his coursework. Blake's account demonstrates how significant these early experiences were, not just in the traditional sense of scaffolding literacy development but also in instilling values and beliefs that would continue to determine his assumptions about his students and his expectations as a teacher. That Blake had trouble "wrap[ping] his mind around" a different view of reading also demonstrates how naturalized these views became and thus the difficulty of letting them go, even when they're no longer helpful.

If Jordi's, Garrett's, and Blake's narratives are any indication, cultural literacy is a conception of literacy powerfully present among literature PhD students, and it is one that is internalized early on. In many ways, it makes them ideal scholars because they are willing to take on difficult texts and spend a great deal of time scrutinizing and mastering them. However, this conception can also be limiting when it comes to teaching writing.

JORDI AND BLAKE IN THE CLASSROOM: THE TEACHING OBSERVATIONS

The graduate instructors whose primary conception of literacy was cultural literacy tended to spend more time on textual interpretation than on writing in their classes and perceived texts and reading to be central to their work as educators, a trend I depict in table 3.2. I differentiate between activities in

Table 3.2. Time spent on discussion of readings and constructive activities aimed at interpretation as a percentage of each participant's total class time observed

Participant	Discipline	Reading— discussion, %	Reading— constructive, %	All reading, %
Blake	literature	80.0	0.0	80.0
Jordi	literature	33.0	38.5	71.5
Garrett	literature	70.0	0.0	70.0
Lily	comp/rhet	32.5	30.0	62.5
Max	creative writing	20.0	20.0	40.0
Barbara	creative writing	22.5	12.5	35.0
Karen	comp/rhet	0.0	17.5	17.5

which students were discussing reading (mostly in large groups, although Blake also had students do this in small groups) and constructive reading activities that also involved writing and were aimed at helping students interpret texts. An example of the latter is an activity, described in what follows, in which Jordi's students created posters advertising the West after reading treatises by C. W. Dana and Theodore Roosevelt.

The fact that I only observed two classes (for a total of three hours and twenty minutes of observation per graduate instructor) makes the results I display in table 3.2 open to scrutiny. However, it is noteworthy that even on the days the other graduate instructors (not Blake, Jordi, or Garrett) were devoting to readings, they also had students writing and working on specific writing skills in class. In addition, these results are supported by statements made by the graduate instructors, as well as other scholarship (see, for example, Blau 2017; Cole and Lyon 2008).

Because Jordi, Garrett, and Blake felt pressure to "cover" the *readings* on the standard syllabus, they all admitted to neglecting writing in their courses. To be clear, Jordi, Garrett, and Blake were troubled that they seemed to be talking about the content of the readings (which I would distinguish from *teaching* reading) more than they talked about writing. Although they wanted to incorporate more writing, because they thought that texts were important and because their own past instruction had focused more on discussing literature, they felt unprepared for the differing curricular goals of the composition classroom, even with the support structure of the practicum.

In addition to the *amount* of reading, the *approach* to reading Jordi, Blake, and Garrett encouraged in their classrooms emphasized close reading of the texts, almost to the exclusion of activities that helped students develop personal connections or bring background knowledge to the experience of reading. (Although Jordi often asked students to make personal connections to texts, she saw this more as indulging students than as a pedagogical tool to bring them closer to the texts they read.) Finally, texts were often a touchstone for their own sense of control and teacherly authority in the classroom. Below, I address these challenges in more depth, focusing on Jordi's and Blake's classes.

Jordi and the Centrality of the Text

Jordi stated that her main learning goal for her students was that they understand and be prepared to "challenge" and "question" the texts they were reading, which on the surface seems counter to her more reverent view of texts (pers. comm., November 18, 2010). In the first class I observed, Jordi asked her students to find quotes from Butler's (2003) *Kindred* that related to the concept of home. She demonstrated taking a sheet of notebook paper and folding it in half lengthwise and then asked the students to write their quotes on the left-hand side of the piece of the paper. On the right-hand side, they were to put their analysis of the quote. The positive aspect of this activity is that it is constructive—rather than lecturing students on how to analyze a quote, Jordi gave them the opportunity to do it themselves so they were constructing meaning and doing something they could use to write their papers.

Yet, Jordi's emphasis on understanding the text also appeared related to her separation of student texts from more privileged creations. She complained that her students were "incapable of analyzing quotes," and because so much of what she saw literacy's being about was hermeneutics, she needed to rectify (or perhaps "remedy") this inability in her classroom (pers. comm., November 18, 2010). In an earlier interview, she had pointed to a sharp contrast between her composition students and the English majors she was used to teaching as a grader and discussion-section leader (pers. comm., October 8, 2010). As I discuss later, her assumptions about students' capabilities point to the presence of "dominant discourses of disability and ability" in her literacy conception (Vidali 2008, 42). That is, inherent in conceptions that value (even implicitly) hierarchy are deficit models and "diagnosis of literate 'ability'" (Dolmage 2008, 15). Jordi at other points showed tremendous care for her students, and the amount of time she spent planning engaging, constructive classes attests to her desire to do right by them. Yet she also was annoyed that her students didn't always do their reading or appear to have the same interpretive skills as the upper-level English majors she was used to.

The second time I observed Jordi's class, her students were examining historical documents that offered differing perspectives on the American West. In the final part of class, her students made posters advertising the West from the perspective of one of these texts. The students had such a good time making their posters that Jordi had to hurry along one of the groups who was putting too much detail into the visual part of the advertisement. Yet during the activity, Jordi indicated she wanted her students to be focusing more on the texts than they were. The following interaction happened as Jordi was circulating around the classroom to give her students pointers and ask questions about their advertisements. She stopped at the group who was supposed to be advertising the West from the perspective of C. W. Dana.

STUDENT 1: Who is the audience for our ad?

STUDENT 2: Our audience is . . .

JORDI: According to Dana . . . look at the text.

STUDENT 1: Oh.

STUDENT 2: It's . . .

JORDI: Look at the text, the text is your source for this. (field notes, March 14, 2011)

In this exchange, the importance of the text becomes paramount for Jordi. She wants her students to look at the text as they work on the posters, even to quote phrases from it. When we discussed this moment in our interview, Jordi said, "When I do get creative, I feel like I end up not connecting it to the texts as well, in specific ways, as I should. You know, so . . . making them come up with a quote from the text would be good to incorporate" (pers. comm., March 14, 2011). I pointed out that the group had included the phrase "the land of milk and honey," which Dana refers to in his essay, in their advertisement. She responded,

> I feel like that they might not have really known where that came from, or what it meant, or, you know I don't want to give like a Bible class, but . . . I kept reminding them, this isn't just an ad, this is based on the text, but like pushing them to do that. So if I could require . . . like you need to have a quote.

Here, Jordi worries that her students don't possess the cultural knowledge to recognize biblical allusions. Her goal of getting them to use the text also seems rooted in a desire to manage the activity—that without a requirement to include a quote, she cannot enforce the close adherence to texts she deems essential to their development as readers and writers. Notably, she does not interpret students' excitement about the activity (which she also mentions) as a sign of its success. Rather, success is measured in terms of students' adherence to the text.

Jordi's grappling to justify her focus on texts suggests the need to create spaces in the practicum to come to terms with what it means to place so much importance on one dimension of the literacy experience. Jordi said later in the interview, "I mean, of course we're working with texts. We read books. Like, this is what we do" (pers. comm., March 14, 2011). When I pressed her to continue with this thought, she replied,

Umm . . . because if the text weren't there, what would we be doing? Because a discussion has to start somewhere? Because ideas are important? I don't know. I mean, that's a really hard question, and it's definitely something I take for granted. Like, the text is the thing. That's where you start.

Jordi starts by taking the emphasis on the text to be a given without questioning it. However, the "I don't know" signals a turning point at which she realizes she must question the ideas about literacy she has taken for granted. Jordi then admits, "It's almost . . . like I get so caught up with making sure they understand the readings that then it's an afterthought, that they need to know how to write about them." In this case, the danger of focusing so heavily on the text is that it can take precedence over any other kind of activity, including activities in which students create their own meaning. Here, Jordi begins to interrogate her approach and why it might not be the best way to teach writing, demonstrating the advantages of creating opportunities for graduate instructors to understand their literacy worldviews. In our interview, Jordi started to grasp the telos behind her literacy assumptions, marking a point where she could finally begin to see—and perhaps begin the painful process of letting go of—views she had held for the greater part of her life.

Blake's Classes: Close Reading and New Criticism

Garrett's and Blake's classes were both dominated by discussion of texts and instructor-led close reading. Both knew they wanted students to understand the text and that they couldn't just give them the interpretation, which would be too close to the kind of "lecture" format critiqued in the practicum. However, they struggled with how to ascertain that students would come up with the "right" interpretation. Blake, whose classes I discuss more in depth here, told me his students had probably struggled with the text and consequently needed his help interpreting it. He stated, "They can't read these essays on their own. There's no question of that . . . they just don't have the reading skills" (pers. comm., November 22, 2010) Blake was right in that many of the composition students did need help interpreting what were difficult readings in genres to which they weren't accustomed. But I also note some of the same ableist assumptions that appeared in Jordi's interviews in terms of what they viewed students as "able" to do. What might be helpful for Blake is a vocabulary for talking about composition students that doesn't see them in terms of deficits or cast them into identities that "are assumed to be in need of fixing"—that is, for situating students' abilities in terms of what they can accomplish with help, as well as acknowledging we all encounter genres we are unfamiliar with and would not be "able" to read independently (Vidali 2008, 46).

Like Jordi, Blake used small groups as a tool for engaging students in the text, a practice recommended in the practicum. In this particular class, each group had a section of the article and was supposed to respond to a question about it. What struck me as I observed, though, was that students were either silent or off task until Blake came around to talk to them. This could be because the class was late in the day or because Blake was right and students needed more resources before he asked them to work in groups. Nevertheless, I got the sense that each group was waiting for Blake to answer the question for them.

Part of the reason for his students' hesitance could be that Blake had signaled to his students that some readings of the text were right while others were wrong.

> BLAKE: Well, we didn't define history yet, and we need to for one of your paper prompts. [*reads from the prompt*] Does anyone know what Janus-faced means?
> STUDENT 1: Two-faced.
> BLAKE: Yeah, it's like there's a dual notion of history. So, what is history? Can someone give me a definition?
> STUDENT 2: Events that happened in the past?
> BLAKE: No, it's not.
> STUDENT 2: Our recollection of the event?
> BLAKE: It's not even that. (field notes, November 22, 2010)

Here, Blake implies his questions have only one answer and thus makes himself the key to understanding the texts. As he moved around the room to check in on his groups, many students responded that they "didn't know" what to do or were "confused." Blake would answer by selecting portions of the text and then explaining them to his students. As he circled among the groups, Blake put a great deal of thought and care into helping his students, not realizing, perhaps, that he had made his own task doubly hard by not giving them more agency and by making assumptions about what they were "able" to do.

When I asked Blake about his decision to break students into small groups to look at the article, he said,

> [The groups] allow me to focus their attention on one particular text that they already read, and read it too quickly and didn't understand it. So I can go back, and I can give them fifteen minutes to focus on something much smaller and shorter. This gives them a little bit more of a chance to actually understand what the text is saying as opposed to simply resaying what I'm saying about the text. And we've got an hour and forty minute class period, which is just massive time to just focus on close reading of a text, so I like to spend some of the time actually rereading it. (pers. comm., November 22, 2010)

In this passage, Blake repeats the word "text" four times and foregrounds the importance of critical interpretation. However, he struggles with coming up with a way to make *students'* interpretation happen. It is telling, as well, how Blake envisions the possibilities for spending the "massive" amount of class time allotted. Either students can "focus on close reading" or they can reread. The possibility that they could also be writing does not, in this moment, seem to occur to him.

Blake's class was similarly focused on the text the next time I visited, this time in the spring semester. After class, I asked Blake directly about his focus on texts and close reading. He responded,

> I'm not sure how well it [close reading] works with this syllabus. When I was an undergrad, my composition course . . . was all literature. . . . So, I'm not really one hundred percent sure how to treat this differently, but I'm definitely teaching it as a literature course, even though almost everything we're reading is an essay,

or an argument. There may be another way to teach it, but I've never taken a course that . . . focused on texts like these. (pers. comm., February 28, 2011)

Blake's explanation echoes sentiments I have heard elsewhere from other graduate students coming from literary studies backgrounds: close reading and literature are what they know, what they've experienced, and what they feel comfortable with. Even with the practicum there to support him, Blake had to fill up many a class period largely by himself, and the way that felt natural and comfortable was to teach what he knows.

Blake modeled his composition course on a literature course he had taken as an undergraduate taught by his "favorite professor." He recounted,

> She was really the professor who taught me how to write. So, I got on in her classes fairly well. She didn't do anything terribly out of the ordinary. She just led discussions on the texts we were reading, and she did it very well. Somehow, I just thrived there. (pers. comm., November 1, 2010)

Earlier in his interview, he referenced the same teacher, describing her as "brilliant." He said,

> Her approach . . . is that she doesn't read five pages of drivel. So she tells all her students that, whatever essay they hand in has to fit on one page and that a quality paper is going to be size-nine font, which she says is the smallest she can read . . . single-spaced with no margins. . . . And she says an "A" paper ought to be that, but if it's not an "A" paper then she would much rather it be a one-page paper than, well, four pages of nothing in five hundred words. So, this is the format that she actually asked for, and . . . I'm going to adopt that myself, eventually.

I was taken aback by Blake's reasoning for his instructor's not wanting to read more than a page of a student's text, especially his description of student papers as "drivel," as it posits a less-than-favorable view of student texts. I don't think Blake meant (at least not directly) to insult his students by saying this—after all, he himself was included in this mandate to condense his paper to a single page. Rather, his response points to the influence past teachers can have on new graduate instructors as they invent themselves as teachers. In this instance, however, the influence was a hindering one—and one I argue Blake would have to resituate or get past in order to be able to help students whose backgrounds and experiences were different from his.

Even though I am asserting here that Blake needed more resources to help him come to a different understanding of his students' literacy practices, I also think the practicum was pushing him to identify problems with the kind of classroom his literature teacher had modeled. Although he still found text-centered approaches to teaching composition compelling, he also had moments in which he questioned whether close reading really worked for a composition class. I asked him about his philosophy towards texts and close reading towards the end of our final interview.

> ME: Okay, so I guess that using texts, analyzing a text . . . that's something that's very important to you?
>
> BLAKE: Yeah. Um, I don't know that there's any other way to . . . is analyzing a text that someone else wrote a very different skill from analyzing a text that you wrote, and if you can analyze a text you wrote then you're . . . ?
>
> ME: Why do you think it's important for students to analyze texts?
>
> BLAKE: To teach them how to write. So, if they can analyze a text, then they can produce a text. (pers. comm., February 28, 2011)

As Jordi did in our interview, Blake foregrounds textual analysis as the basis for literacy, and, in a way, he's right. He was, after all, teaching a very specialized, academic literacy, which is centered on texts and text production. But Blake might also have had difficulty imagining a writing course in which students use other forms of evidence or data, an approach to writing that, as Erika Lindemann (1993) argues, acknowledges that "interpreting texts . . . represents only one way of knowing" (314; see also Howard 2014). Blake relied, in his teaching, on the rich set of resources he brought with him, including a life steeped in texts and learning. However, it would also be beneficial to have experiences in which he could see writing and literacy across or beyond the disciplines, challenging him to expand his view of what counts as literacy in FYC.

CONCLUSION: MOVING BEYOND THE "TEXT ITSELF"

Throughout this chapter, I point to individual and institutional sponsors that reinforced Jordi's, Garrett's, and Blake's sense of literacy as textual interpretation. I also show why these influences were so compelling for these three, derived as they were from early family-based experiences and then reinforced through later schooling and cultural conceptions and myths about literacy, including what Ruth Finnegan (1973) describes as a "Great Divide" conception that places those who have certain, privileged literacies in a position of dominance over those who do not.

Yet, I also want to emphasize that these tacit hierarchical beliefs were not mean spirited or purposively exclusionary. Rather, Jordi, Garrett, and Blake all described their preference for teaching students to interpret texts over teaching writing in terms of comfort and familiarity. In her response to an activity for which I asked them to rank different writing assignments (see appendix C), Jordi stated,

> These rankings reflect my somewhat tenuous belief in the important of the text. . . . While I value the concept of relating text to self and text to world, I think establishing such relationships is difficult or superficial without first establishing a deep understanding of the text itself. For this reason, I've ranked assignments that center on the ideas in the text before asking students to relate those ideas to the space outside the text.

Besides her repetition of "text" six times, Jordi also seems to think of the text as a safe place, a training ground or harbor before students venture out into the "space outside the text." Her response recalls Blake's assertion that he was more "comfortable" teaching the last unit of the composition course because he was teaching literature. When I asked him more about this, he said, "Um, with literature, I'm a little bit more accustomed

for myself where the evidence is . . . it's a little less off the wall"
(pers. comm., November 1, 2010). He explained:

> This is basically New Criticism, and undergrads mostly write New
> Criticism from what I can tell. So it is a more contained body of
> evidence. . . . I wonder if that's a difference between disciplines
> where, in English, if we can restrict ourselves to the body of evi-
> dence of one text, we can let students be a little more free, as far
> as picking what they want to argue about or argue for.

Blake was the only one of the graduate instructors to explicitly
mention New Criticism (although Jordi's reference above to
"the text itself" also appears influenced by it), and in this statement he also articulates a central New Critical assumption: iron-
ically, by restricting students to this text, we are letting them "be
a little more free." Garrett also referred to literature as a familiar space, saying (of a paper he wrote on *Finnegan's Wake*), "I
know I'm in the living room because it's literature, and because
I have some familiarity there" (pers. comm., October 20, 2010).
This comfort with literature became a touchstone for these
three as they ventured into the unfamiliar world of teaching.

Yet I also point throughout this chapter to fissures in these
graduate instructors' conceptions, or openings where they
began to reconsider their literacy views. During our initial
interview, Garrett confided that he thought the "veil" separat-
ing him from his grandmother was "bullshit in some way" and
that he and his grandmother (as well as his current students)
were "all climbing the same hill" (pers. comm., October 20,
2010). Garrett rightly saw literacy's use in gatekeeping, as well
as his own complicity in this system due to his decision to pursue a graduate degree in English. But despite how compelling
this view of literacy as gatekeeper is, he also indicated his desire
for spaces where he could reconsider it. Although Jordi wasn't
ready to recognize hierarchical views in herself, she did see
them in her English-professor father. She told me that even as
she was following in his footsteps, she wanted to put more effort
into her teaching than he did, and this effort showed in her
teaching, in which she was creating opportunities for students
to engage with texts and produce meaning.

Conceptions of literacy are so ingrained and so close to us that we often don't see them until, as one reviewer for this book put it, they become a source of tension because they reveal some inadequacy in ourselves, our students, or our teaching. Jordi recognized she needed a fuller consideration of literacy and what it means to teach writing, stating,

> Practicum is just weird because it's like I've never thought about my writing before. . . . You would think that you think about your writing. And how you write and why you write as an English person, but at least I haven't really. . . . I can think critically about the world but not about my own writing [*laughs*]. (pers. comm., October 26, 2010)

Jordi's admission demonstrates that the kind of close, critical reading new graduate instructors in literary studies have been engaged in does not necessarily translate to a similar critical distance in terms of reading and reflecting on their past experiences. Introducing new graduate instructors to the insights of literacy studies can push them to interrogate the *why* of what they're doing. Literacy studies is uniquely positioned to help graduate instructors awaken to the broadened possibilities literacy (as opposed to just literature) offers. Jody Shipka (2013) states, referencing curricular goals in composition, "What matters is not simply '*that*' students in our courses learn to produce a specific kind of text . . . but that students leave our courses exhibiting *a more nuanced* awareness of the various choices they make throughout the process of accomplishing that work and the effect those choices might have on others" (76). The same could be said of the (admittedly overburdened) role of the composition practicum. But given that many of the attitudes described by the graduate instructors here were also reinforced elsewhere in their graduate program, work in the practicum toward helping graduate instructors recognize their conceptions of literacy—and their effects on teaching—must happen in conjunction with broader changes to the culture of English studies so it is more inclusive of diverse literate practices.

Part of incorporating more diverse understandings of literacy could also include drawing more on the critical insights

of disability studies in creating curricula to support graduate instructors throughout their professional development.
Although scholarship on disability has been incorporated into
fields like composition, literature, and education (to name
only a few), for new graduate instructors, disability theory, even
when taught in practica or graduate seminars, might seem separate from their teaching unless they have students with disabilities that are easy to see. In fact, many of Jordi's, Garrett's, and
Blake's statements about what they thought students weren't
"able" to do occurred right after the practicum class in which
they discussed readings by Jay Dolmage (2008) and Amy Vidali
(2008). As Vidali (2008) demonstrates, disability studies' challenge of "the medical model" and "deficit models," often
invoked when talking not only about students in basic writing classes but also in classes not designated as such, can help
instructors develop more informed understandings of composition students' "abilities" (43). But the practicum class might
not have sufficiently prompted the graduate instructors to use
"disability as insight" into thinking about students without obvious disabilities (43).

Practica could also invite graduate instructors like Jordi,
Blake, and Garrett into a deeper understanding of the literate
practices they value by asking them to model a lesson on an
activity, like close reading, they feel comfortable with. During
the course of this activity, practica instructors would demonstrate that there are aspects of intensive reading activities like
close reading that can be valuable, while also moving graduate instructors away from narrow, New Critical versions of close
reading that don't value aspects of literacy (like reader and context) crucial to teaching reading. Assigning graduate instructors to model lessons would be a way of engaging their funds of
knowledge while also putting their conceptions of literacy into
productive conflict.

In the spring following these graduate instructors' first semester of teaching, I was talking to David about text-centric views
of literacy and the role of the practicum in helping graduate instructors think through their literacy views. David was

familiar with Welch's (1993) article arguing against the practicum as a site for conversion, and though the cultural-literacy view seemed the most worrisome of the literacy conceptions, David also stated, "I don't really want to convert anybody. I just want to expand their senses of possibility" (pers. comm., January 24, 2011). That is, despite the deep anxieties many in composition have about the cultural-literacy views of some instructors, we can envision ways for our instructor-educating programs to intervene without forcing graduate instructors through an assembly line or presenting composition pedagogy as a monolith in which only some views are acceptable. In the next chapter, I discuss implications of current discussions about composition's disciplinarity in light of this balance between exposing new graduate instructors to what compositionists "know" and engaging their literacy preconceptions.

4

GRADUATE INSTRUCTORS AT THE THRESHOLD
Threshold Concepts, Disciplinarity, and Social/Critical Literacy

Until we develop and act from principles about the meaning of what composition and writing studies is as a discipline, and then link what happens in composition courses—which exist within our discipline—to those principles, we are at the mercy of the companies seeking to keep our company.

—Linda Adler-Kassner

In the spring of 2017, I sat in a crowded ballroom at the Conference on College Composition and Communication's annual convention for a session titled "Naming What WE Know: A Roundtable on Knowledge Production in Composition" organized by Jason Alexander, Eli Goldblatt, Angela Haas, Paula Mathieu, and Jacqueline Rhodes. The larger purpose of the panel was to challenge the normative "we" in Linda Adler-Kassner and Elizabeth Wardle's (2015) *Naming What We Know: Threshold Concepts of Writing Studies*. Rhodes argued, for example, that she was troubled by the "we" of the book. Stating her feelings of exclusion from the disciplinary concepts named, and in particular the exclusion of queer theory and queerness in relation to identity, she stated, "I'm not here." Speakers also pointed to the finality of print for articulating concepts in flux. Finally, as Goldblatt argued, the book seems to narrow the focus of our field from literacy (which also includes reading, nonacademic literacies, community-based literacies, etc.) to academic writing.

DOI: 10.7330/9781607329343.c004

Adler-Kassner and Wardle's book, and the responses to it, say much about our field's current sense of its disciplinary identity. As Yancey (2015) argues in the book's introduction, "The assumption underlying *Naming*, of course, is that *the field is now established*" (xxix; emphasis mine). The "threshold concepts," which are positioned as the central knowledge of disciplinary experts in composition, and their accompanying analyses thus convey a sense of finality and discipline-wide consensus. Elsewhere, as the epigraph above indicates, Adler-Kassner (2012) has noted the urgency of the larger project of naming (and asserting) what composition, as a field, has come to "know" about writing, elaborating that if we don't do the work of defining what writing studies is and does, "there are plenty of people who will do it for us" (135).

The rush to claim composition and rhetoric's (or writing studies') disciplinary status and to articulate clearly what compositionists have come to know over the past fifty or so years is thus both real and understandable. Even within our own departments, as I argue elsewhere, the teaching of composition is still often stigmatized and our expertise called into question (see Brewer and di Gennaro 2018). At my current institution, the conviction that composition is a "service" discipline still inflects the ways decisions are made and resources are allocated. For example, a few years ago, the university's Academic Conduct Committee completed an overhaul of the Academic Integrity Code without consulting any of the writing specialists on campus about how plagiarism should be defined. However, the committee also expected the composition program to include information about the new code in workshops for composition faculty and require faculty to show a PowerPoint presentation about the new code in all composition courses. So while we were not included in decision-making, we were expected to be central players for implementation.

I can thus well appreciate Yancey's (2018) statement that "without a clear articulation of what we know," the field of composition and rhetoric is "vulnerable" (29). Jennifer Helene Maher (2018) further describes what she terms an "institutionalized denial of disciplinary expertise" at her university, which "affects a whole range of other issues," including "first-year composition pedagogy, vertical curriculum scaffolding," graduate-instructor education, hiring, and class size (173). I agree with these scholars that in our departments and in our larger colleges, universities, and academic communities our expertise must be recognized and acknowledged and that full disciplinarity gives us, at the very least, a better seat at the table.

Of course, declarations about our disciplinary maturity are nothing new; fifteen years ago, Ede (2004) stated in her influential *Situating Composition*, "Composition has achieved if not full disciplinarity then something remarkably close to it" (x). Yet, Ede also (appropriately) situates that reach for disciplinarity within the context of what the field of composition and rhetoric has needed to do at certain points of our history to be perceived as a legitimate "scholarly enterprise in the eyes of our colleagues" (56; see also Goldblatt 2017).

Although the work of composition is arguably much more central to most English departments now, challenges from disciplinary outsiders who claim to "speak for writing" still rankle and tread heavily on our own scholarly and institutional identities (Adler-Kassner 2018, 310). Yet I think we must also question what it means to proclaim that we have a "disciplinary core" and what effect that core has on the professionalization of graduate students, both within our field and outside. As Yancey (2015) asks in her introduction to *Naming*, "What of any of . . . [these threshold concepts] do we share with our students, when, and how?" (xviii). However, in *Naming* and in Rita Malenczyk, Susan Miller-Cochran, Elizabeth Wardle, and Kathleen Blake Yancey's (2018) *Composition, Rhetoric, and Disciplinarity*, discussions of what threshold concepts (as well as our sense of disciplinary maturity) mean for graduate-teacher education have largely been absent.

Kristen Hansen's (2018) chapter in *Composition, Rhetoric, and Disciplinarity* comes perhaps the closest to considering what the increased urgency surrounding composition's disciplinarity might mean for the education of new graduate instructors.

Citing the reality that many (if not most) institutions are likely to continue to rely mostly on graduate students and adjuncts to staff their courses, she asks, "Do first-time teachers always have to be the greenest of novices? Do we have to content ourselves with getting them only to the stage of advanced beginner before they leave?" (146). Her answer, that "we as a discipline and a profession *insist*" on a minimum (much more robust than we currently have) of coursework for new teachers, points to the urgency and importance of graduate-instructor education in the context of composition's legitimacy as a discipline (149; emphasis mine).

But given the importance of new graduate instructors' preconceptions as they take in their teacher education and teach for the first time, I also argue that assertions of our disciplinarity must not only reflect a broader sense of what composition is than what is currently suggested in *Naming* but also must present the conceptions about writing (and literacy) valued by our field in ways that are accessible and nonthreatening to newcomers. Given how varied new graduate instructors' conceptions of literacy are (as well as the variety in their levels of experience and willingness to commit to the difficult, developmental work of learning composition pedagogy), this process will likely have to be individualized for each new graduate instructor.

In this chapter, I define threshold concepts and consider their relationship with disciplinarity and graduate-teacher education through case studies of Barbara and Max, the two focal participants whose field was creative writing. Like the literature PhD students, these two could thus be considered disciplinary outsiders, and, like all the graduate instructors in this study, they were certainly novices when it came to teaching composition. And yet, while many of the graduate instructors I observed had moments of dissonance in their encounters with the readings for the practicum and the concepts informing the FYWP at Public, this dissonance was much less pronounced for Barbara and Max because they came to their first semester of teaching with understandings of literacy already in line with some of the fundamental assumptions of composition pedagogy. These two felt a sense of validation and even exhilaration when they began to read composition theory because it gave voice to ideas they already had and opened up opportunities for thinking about literacy in ways they were already attuned to.

Like the experiences of graduate instructors presented in previous chapters, Barbara's and Max's experiences work against the archetype of the resistant graduate student, pointing to new ways to conceptualize graduate instructors' early experiences with composition pedagogy. Further, Max's and Barbara's position as MFA students teaching FYW speaks to the issue of disciplinarity in that often there is an assumption that it is the graduate students in composition and rhetoric programs who are automatically better (or at least more committed) teachers of writing. I had expected Max's and Barbara's beliefs, as MFA students, to be more like Lily's and Karen's: writing is personal and expressive and, therefore, can't be taught. While it certainly may be the case that many creative writing MFAs do think of writing in more Romantic terms, trends in experimental poetry, in fiction and creative nonfiction for political and social change, and in challenging traditional genres and modes for composing may mean more personal, expressive conceptions of literacy among creative writing MFAs aren't a given.

The realization that these two creative writing MFA students did not necessarily think of writing in individual, expressive terms is significant because a large proportion of the FYWP graduate instructors are creative writers, a trend noted by other scholars (Goldblatt 2017; Hesse 2010). At Public, the overall makeup of the practicum course was over half (ten out of eighteen) creative writing MFAs. To return to Hansen's (2018) questions, it remains the case that whereas comp/rhet graduate students will have continued opportunities to revisit their teaching in light of future study in composition theory, this opportunity may not emerge for creative writing MFAs unless they actively seek it out. Nevertheless, understanding how to support graduate students (and faculty) in creative writing is an ever-present issue for many WPAs, and Barbara's and Max's experiences reveal ways of engaging creative writing MFAs in composition theory.

At the same time, Barbara's and Max's experiences also demonstrate that socializing new graduate instructors into a particular view does not automatically make their first year of teaching trouble free. That is, the process of learning composition pedagogy is a long and complex one, even when graduate instructors' ideologies align more neatly with that of their formal education in pedagogy. I begin by defining the conception of literacy that most closely matches the views of Barbara and Max: social/critical literacy. I then change angles somewhat to examine Barbara's and Max's experiences with the pedagogy presented in the practicum in terms of the threshold concepts described in *Naming*. I end the chapter by reconsidering how the conceptions of literacy of graduate instructors in the study informing this book might speak to the current discussions about threshold concepts and disciplinarity in composition.

DEFINING SOCIAL/CRITICAL LITERACY

Goggin (2008) defines social/critical literacy as the conception that recognizes literacy as being "ideologically situated in social contexts" (70). As the name hints, it has two related theoretical components. The first is a view of language as social and of literacy as the means with which people create relationships with others. The second is that it is ideological and thus open to questions of who is speaking from what position and why. From this ideological understanding of language also comes the contention that literacy has had a role in sustaining social, political, and institutional relationships structured so as to give one group power over another. In some instances, those with this view look to literacy as the means for marginalized groups to shift these power relationships and challenge the social or political elite (Scribner 1984, 11). In this light, this conception of literacy can have political and activist components as well. It encompasses both social-constructivist (e.g., Kenneth Bruffee, Patricia Bizzell, and David Bartholomae) and critical-pedagogy views (e.g., Paulo Freire and Ira Shor).

Social/critical literacy in composition has come to imply a range of theoretical and pedagogical goals. However, the figure Knoblauch (1990) and Goggin (2008) cite as the exemplar for this conception is Freire (2008), whose idea of *conscientização*, or "critical consciousness," is the central theoretical principle behind critical pedagogy (35). In Freire's (2008) view, to become critically conscious is to go beyond naivety and the "culture of silence" that makes oppressed groups internalize the negative views of their oppressors (30). Compositionists and others have interpreted critical consciousness more expansively as a way of using texts (figured broadly), writing, and literate practices to examine and think critically about language and the world.

From a practical perspective, views of literacy that foreground its social role also recognize that a number of public perspectives of the composition course, including the idea that it can function as a one-shot inoculation to teach students some sort of universally "good" writing, are misguided because writing is always situated. Doug Downs (2016) argues, in fact, that the composition course itself is defined by these "competing senses of its purpose" (51). That is, FYC exists by virtue of this tension between what public stakeholders think it is (a "how-to course centered on grammar instruction") and how compositionists have conceptualized it (50–51). It should be noted too that compositionists' senses of composition pedagogy are also divergent, as the twelve writing pedagogies described in Gary Tate, Amy Rupiper, Kurt Schick, and H. Brooke Hessler's (2013) *Guide to Composition Pedagogies* make evident (see also Smit 2004).

The divergent and multifaceted nature of composition pedagogy is thus likely to be confusing for novice instructors, especially those who expect teaching to be straightforward and/or to align neatly with their preconceptions of writing and writing pedagogy. And although I agree with David Smit (2004) and others that there has been a lack of consensus about what FYC should entail, I also argue that the concept of writing (and thus literacy) as social, situated, and rhetorical can be seen as a thread throughout these pedagogies, even some expressivist and process pedagogies. Yet because social/critical conceptions of literacy go against cultural commonplaces, they are likely to be alien to some new graduate instructors. For example, although none of the graduate instructors at Public subscribed to a view of the course as teaching only (or even mostly) grammar, many of them believed in a universal writing (often defined as clear and concise writing). Moreover, as discussed in chapters 2 and 3, social/critical conceptions of literacy may be difficult for graduate instructors more attuned to the individual or text-based facets of the literacy experience.

THRESHOLD CONCEPTS AND SOCIAL/CRITICAL LITERACY

The graduate instructors' difficulty in grappling with social/critical literacy conceptions, then, fit well within current understandings of threshold concepts. Although the threshold concepts for the field of composition don't all necessarily reflect social/critical literacy views, their initially troublesome, even threatening qualities make them relevant to the experiences of new graduate instructors as they encounter social/critical views in their teacher education. As Adler-Kassner, John Majewski, and Damian Koshnick (2012) clarify, quoting education researcher David Perkins, threshold concepts "can be 'counter-intuitive, alien . . . or incoherent' because they challenge existing beliefs, past practices or inert knowledge, or can be conceptually difficult." Threshold concepts also challenge learners to reflect on tacit knowledge of which they are "only peripherally aware or entirely unconscious" (Perkins 2006, 40; see also Meyer and Land 2006, 9–14).

Also relevant to the experiences of new graduate instructors is that threshold concepts are "liminal" (Adler-Kassner, Majewski, and Koshnick 2012). As Adler-Kassner, Majewski, and Koshnick (2012) state, "They are 'portals' through which learners must pass," and, once they pass through the portal, they are transformed. While this transformative potential can seem initially attractive from a teacher-education perspective (we do, after all, want to affect graduate instructors' views, knowledge base, and even, as Dryer [2012] argues, identity), research on graduate-teacher education also demonstrates the difficult and developmental nature of this transformation (Dryer 2012; Reid, Estrem, and Belcheir 2012; Restaino 2012; Welch 1993). Moreover, as evidence from the current study demonstrates, the conceptions with which literacy graduate instructors come to their teacher education will make their experiences with and understanding of threshold concepts more or less difficult. WPAs must, then, offer multiple angles on and avenues into the threshold concepts.

An additional difficulty (and one recently acknowledged by Adler-Kassner and Wardle [2016]) is that new graduate instructors not only must wrestle with threshold concepts of writing (or literacy), they must also learn threshold concepts of *teaching*, making the "portals" they must pass through perhaps more akin to labyrinths. The alien and counterintuitive nature of the threshold concepts is perhaps best illustrated by the previous two chapters, which describe how the graduate instructors who viewed literacy as either largely individual and personal or as more text-centric and cultural struggled with many of the readings and teaching concepts presented in the practicum. Karen's initial experience with the Jarratt (2003) reading, described in chapter 2, illustrates how difficult it is to come to terms with concepts (like Jarratt's argument that instructors must challenge students with sexist and racist views) that violate our conceptions of literacy (like Karen's idea that teachers should be nurturing or open to others' views).

In contrast to the last two chapters, in this chapter I describe the views of the graduate instructors that largely aligned with both social/critical literacy and some of the threshold concepts described in *Naming*. The following sections are thus anchored by four of the threshold concepts from *Naming*. In organizing the following sections in this way, I offer individual, novice takes on these concepts, exploring what they may mean for individuals in the context of their past experiences with literacy.

Barbara: From "the Heating Vent to the Real World"
(Threshold Concept: Writing Is a Social and Rhetorical Activity)
Barbara, a second-year student in the creative writing MFA program, was a fiction writer in her midtwenties who was on the verge of discovering a new love for teaching. I first talked with her when she stayed behind after one of the practicum sessions to ask David what she should do about students who weren't attending class or turning in paper drafts on time. After our initial exchange, Barbara frequently sought me out for advice about her teaching, and we developed a relationship in which she seemed to feel comfortable sharing her ideas and anxieties about teaching.

Barbara had the longest history at Public University because she had earned her undergraduate degree there. Before that she had attended a public high school about half an hour southwest of Public University. She then attended another college in the area before transferring to Public. She was the only one of the focal participants, other than Blake, to have taken a first-year writing course.

The most important thing for Barbara in her quest to become a writing teacher was feeling like part of a community of writers and teachers. She, more than any of the other graduate instructors in the study, sought out extra teaching support when she needed it. She also told me about an online writing community she had joined before graduate school, where she could share her writing and get a sense of how her audience might respond to it. Barbara looked for guidance from the professors teaching her graduate seminars, although at some points she felt rebuffed by them. In short, Barbara was trying hard to make graduate school and teaching, both of which could be isolating, into supportive, communal experiences.

Perhaps because of her acknowledgement of the presence of other people and communities in her literacy development, Barbara's initial views aligned well with the first threshold concept articulated in *Naming: writing is a social and rhetorical activity* (Roozen 2015b, 17). That is, Barbara had already internalized the view that "writers are always doing the rhetorical work of addressing the needs and interests of a particular audience" and that, regardless of how isolating the act of writing may appear to be, "writers draw upon many other people" (17).

The concept of literacy as a social phenomenon emerged clearly during our first interview. Barbara described the experience of writing a paper on the suburbs versus the city in *Howard's End* for one of her graduate seminars, saying,

> I was the only creative writing student in that literature class, and I felt very intimidated and very aware that, you know, I wasn't accepted into graduate school on the basis of a critical paper that I'd written. So I was just very insecure and anxious, but the professor I had was really encouraging to me and said that my comments in class were great. So that really helped, and . . . I kept going to her office hours, and she would help me brainstorm an actual thesis for a paper. (pers. comm., October 22, 2010)

This professor provided just the kind of communal, supportive experience with literacy Barbara craved, and Barbara acknowledges the professor's role as a collaborator with her on the paper. The professor acted as what Brandt (1998) describes as a "literacy sponsor," someone within the institution who authorizes both her writing and her presence in the graduate program.

Barbara contrasted this experience with another professor with whom she felt unable to connect.

> I went to her office hours, and . . . I'm such a people person that if someone's not warm or effusive at all, I just kind of shut down, and I'm like, well . . . this professor doesn't like me . . . she doesn't want to have a relationship with me. You know, it's all about that relationship thing. (pers. comm., October 22, 2010)

Barbara's view of her own writing acknowledges that it draws upon the relationships and contexts within which she is working. The last sentence in the excerpt is representative of her conception of literacy: that it is "all about" relationships.

As we continued to discuss her paper, Barbara began to put her experiences with these professors in the context of Bartholomae's (1985) "Inventing the University," which she had read for the practicum a little over a month prior. In the following exchange, I asked her about her use of "I" in the paper:

> Um, that was probably me trying to invent the university. I remember going to Professor Shenoy with drafts and wanting her to, to help me with the stylization because it was my first graduate paper, and she was like, "Oh no . . . I don't read seminar papers." Um, but before she pushed it away, she did point to a couple of things, like don't do this, don't do that. So that was probably me just trying to copy the essays, the criticism we had been reading in class. (pers. comm., October 22, 2010)

Barbara demonstrates that it is not just undergraduates who have to invent the university. Although graduate students might have a great deal of experience with academic writing, their writing must become more confident and more indicative of their status as experts than before (perhaps also reflecting the threshold concept that *disciplinary and professional identities are constructed through writing* [Estrem 2015, 55]). Barbara said of writing the paper, "I felt like I was learning a whole new way of writing that I don't feel expert in yet." She noted too that she coped by "copying" the writing of others, demonstrating her awareness that authors borrow traces from the work of others (Porter 1986).

Barbara also describes inventing the university as the ability to take on a more authoritative voice. The concept of having a singular voice has of course been challenged in composition studies, in particular by Royster (1996), who points out that consciously using multiple voices has always been a reality for many people of color (37). As we were talking about a short story she had written, I asked Barbara how the idea of voice played into her writing. She replied,

> I came into grad school expecting to find my voice quote-unquote. . . . I think when I'm writing academically, I feel like I'm adopting someone else's voice, and I'm imitating. . . . And in creative writing . . . there are . . . writers that are really great at just creating these voices, like Katie Smith, with all these different people talking and these different dialects and accents. It's marvelous. A criticism I've gotten for my fiction is that all the characters sound the same in their dialogue, or they have the

same voice. So, I think voice is really important, and I've been trying . . . to break out of my personal Barbara voice and actually [*laughs*] embody other people. (pers. comm., October 22, 2010)

In this excerpt, voice quickly turns into voices. She gives author Katie Smith as an example of someone whose work is multivocal, and it is the univocality of Barbara's writing that becomes its shortcoming. Inherent in Barbara's description of voice is an understanding of language as socially constructed and stratified among a number of centripetal and centrifugal forces, a far cry from the idea of having one "authentic" voice.

In Barbara's revised literacy narrative, she makes the idea of writing as communication, rather than solitary reverie, more apparent. She writes,

> With my bi-yearly visits to my aunt and uncle's house, and the mostly female readers and writers I made friends with on Livejournal, I began to change my perception of reading from a solitary activity to a communal one that, while still done alone, could be an invitation to conversations about books and ideas. After Aunt Lucy, I continued to meet smart and inspiring women, some my age and some older than me, who were reading and writing and trying to figure out how to live. They showed me trails I could model my own path on, and they offered encouragement and comfort to me along the way. ("Literacy Narrative Final" 2010)

Barbara describes an important move away from societal representations of literacy as an individual activity to an understanding of literacy in context. The main difference between her early and final literacy narrative is that she can put a name to the change she is describing. Like Karen and Jordi in previous chapters, she self-consciously makes the move of viewing her literacy experiences through a social lens, thus articulating her solidarity with much of the composition theory she had read in the practicum.

The rest of Barbara's final narrative presents a powerful story of how literacy can shape a life. She concludes, saying,

> Aunt Lucy, Janet, Hilary, Talia, and other women, too many to name here, inspired me as I was coming of age as a writer and

a woman. They shared their writing and their hopes and fears about writing. They pulled books off their shelves for me or made recommendations in their Livejournal entries. Through the glimpses I got of their daily lives, I learned how to live in the world as an artist, a teacher, a feminist, and a goddess ("Aunt Lucy is teaching me how to be a goddess," I used to say). They gave me Anne Sexton, Nicole Krauss, and *Bitch Magazine*. Choices I hadn't known existed and an identity I hadn't dared to claim for myself. ("Literacy Narrative Final" 2010)

Barbara's understanding of identity here is a fluid one—it is something to be claimed, enacted, performed rather than a deep self merely to be discovered. She acknowledges influences instead of figuring herself as the lone hero of the story. Although Barbara would need more time to more fully realize and enact the social nature of literacy in her teaching, the fact that she came to her first semester of teaching with a conception that already acknowledged this social view of literacy made her more open to considering the theory presented in the practicum course.

Barbara also advanced a rhetorical understanding of texts in her class. In her view, literature can forward arguments. She expanded on this idea, saying she was "trying not to just teach . . . [*Kindred*] traditionally as a novel in an English class but keep in mind what the author wanted to say and why they made the choices they made" (pers. comm., November 17, 2010). When I asked her to clarify how she saw teaching a novel in an English class as opposed to teaching it in composition, she explained that her approach had been

> not to look for the red shirts and what does that mean but to just treat it like a text and focus on, you know, what are our expectations? Is there an argument in this text?

Barbara's understanding of a literature as opposed to a composition class, appears, then, to be that the former is isolated in many ways from a world in which we need arguments to do things and effect change, whereas composition is engaged with practical and political concerns. Although this may not be a fair assessment of literature courses, it nonetheless points to a *perception* of literature classes as representing a retreat from, rather than an engagement with, the world. Barbara's comment also characterizes composition classes as developing students' metacognitive and genre awareness; they don't just look at the messages or symbols within a text but rather at how the text creates these and the various decisions authors make. Barbara's background in creative writing influences her to see texts in terms of production, a disposition that makes her more apt to accept building students' meta-awareness of writing as a central goal.

In her graduate seminars as well, Barbara was striving to view literature differently, essentially as a form of rhetoric. She made an important move toward this understanding by engaging in what Reiff and Bawarshi (2011) have labeled "not" talk, in which students "describe their written work (and writing process) by explaining what . . . [it] is not" (325). For Reiff and Bawarshi, a willingness to engage in "not" talk is one of the key moves by which students begin to change their beliefs about writing, as it signals a willingness to reinvent and reimagine past ways of viewing literacy. In the above passages, Barbara says the word "not" twice, implying that her past experiences with literature classes and the ways of interpreting texts she had internalized from these classes were insufficient as pedagogical tools for the composition classroom. In other words, Barbara recognizes that she has what Yancey, Roberston, and Taczak (2014) refer to as "absent prior knowledge" (108). Significantly, it is this lack of confidence in her own ability to know what should constitute a composition course (as opposed to a literature one) that made Barbara more open to trying teaching strategies from the practicum and modifying her prior understandings of literacy to be more in-line with conceptions communicated by the practicum.

Max and Intertextuality (Threshold Concept: Texts Get Their Meaning from Other Texts)

A creative writing student in his early twenties, Max had an easygoing, quirky personality, often chiming in during class discussions with comments that made David and the other graduate instructors laugh. Max was from a suburban community in the Midwest. His mother, at the time of the interview, was not working but had taught preschool and then worked at a health club. His father had been self-employed since Max was in kindergarten and worked in finance. Before that, though, his father had worked as a pipefitter before going back to college and eventually earning a master's degree in geography. Like Garrett (in the last chapter), Max seemed uncomfortable admitting one of his parents had held a blue-collar job. He told me that finding this out "was strange. I didn't even know that about him for a long time, that he was a pipefitter for a few years. He told me that kind of recently, and, um, yeah, it's like interesting" (pers. comm., October 25, 2010). Max's partially working-class background did, however, appear to make him more conscious of the class-based, tiered nature of the university and more empathetic towards students who were first-generation college students, worked significant hours, were veterans, or had children.

Max had attended a public high school, which he described as "the rotten apple of the good school district bunch"; even though it was one of the highest paid districts for teachers, his particular school consistently underperformed (pers. comm., October 25, 2010). He went to college at a state school in the same state where he grew up. Max explained, "I wasn't really sure if I wanted to go to college at all, so I just kind of chose there because it was so close, and it would be convenient if I were to drop out."[1] Max's initial ambivalence about college led him to be more accepting of students in his class who had the same reticence about education.

Like Barbara, Max expressed an understanding of language as always situated. The specific way he described this understanding of language was through the idea of intertextuality. Charles Bazerman (2004) argues that intertextuality recognizes that "texts to do not appear in isolation, but in relation to other texts. We write in response to others" (53). This understanding of literacy, then, recognizes the social, situated nature of texts (considered here broadly) that is fundamental to composition theory. Kevin Roozen (2015a) labels intertextuality a "difficult concept" because it "conflict[s] with dominant Western notions of authorship, creativity and originality" (46; see also Porter 1986). However, for Max, intertextuality was a means for helping his composition students create connections between the texts in the College Composition classroom and their own lives, blurring the lines among text-to-text, text-to-self, and text-to-world connections.

In the FYWP at Public, helping students understand how texts work with and respond to one another is a central literacy goal of their instructors. For Max, this concept made sense as a pedagogical goal because he was able to locate it easily within understandings of literacy he already held. As a poetry MFA student, Max envisioned language as a form of appropriation and argued for a conceptual poetry situated in opposition to Romantic ideas of originality and creativity. Throughout our interview, Max referred to playing with the ideas of plagiarism and appropriation in his poetry.

Our conversation about intertextuality began with a look at two poems Max had composed, both of which play with the conventions of documentation and other textual mechanisms for noting relationships between texts. Max wrote the poems as a response to a debate over whether documentation was necessary in poetry. Although Max acknowledged that one of his goals in playing with citation and even directly copying some lines of his poem from websites was to subvert citation conventions, he also contended that he was trying to point out citation's importance. Max explained,

> I think intertextuality's really important. . . . There's a line in here, "The interwebbing together of everything creative through common textual citations. And, I don't know, that's probably a utopian idea, that everything can somehow be connected, but I think there's some level of truth to that." (pers. comm., October 25, 2010)

Max's idea is commensurate with Bazerman's (2004) (and Mikhail Bakhtin's) description of intertextuality as locating an utterance within a web of other utterances. More important, Max's view of intertextuality makes him recognize the always-situated nature of language, a concept that worked well with understandings of literacy presented by the practicum. Max's view of writing and language as inherently intertextual influenced his desire for his students to make connections among texts as well. He elaborated on this in the following exchange:

> MAX: In this piece I . . . use part of Herman Hesse's *Siddartha*. Um, basically because . . . I just always remember that, this section about where the guy is talking about the river. So, when I was writing this, I was thinking so much about rivers, I had to go dig out my copy of *Siddartha*, and I found that quote, and I put it in there. . . . I just kind of saw that connection and inserted it.
>
> ME: Is that something that you would want your students to do?
>
> MAX: Yeah, like, recall things that you've read. Always be able to make connections between what you're reading and what you have read, what you already know. (pers. comm., October 25, 2010)

Max wants his students to recognize themselves as social beings, connected to and constructed by the texts they have read and, thus, connected even to the readings they might not initially see as relevant to themselves. He also understands and respects that students come to his classroom with their own "funds of knowledge" and sees engaging students' funds of knowledge as part of his role as their teacher (Moll et al., 1992).

Max, Graffiti, and Multimodal Texts (Threshold Concept: All Writing Is Multimodal)

Max also talked about working with images and even writing a paper on graffiti, making his literacy perspective the most overtly multimodal of any of the participants. The concepts that writing is not solely alphanumeric and that composition instructors might engage students using multiple textual modes are, by themselves, probably not either troublesome or conceptually difficult for many new graduate instructors, regardless of disciplinary identity or conception of literacy. The troublesome aspect of this threshold concept is that it conflicts with the following assumptions: first, as Cheryl Ball and Colin Charlton (2015) argue, many people assume multimodal is synonymous with digital, when, in fact, multimodal texts include things like paintings or zines that may or may not be digitally produced (42–3). Second, as Shipka (2013) argues, we should see multimodality not as "some special feature of certain texts, objects, or performances" but rather as a feature of all texts (74). This consideration is important, as it allows composition instructors to think about the inclusion of multiple modes in their classrooms in ways that aren't artificial or tacked on—that is, choosing among modes and experimenting with and acknowledging multimodality are more integrated into students' (and instructors') conceptions of composing.

Max's multimodal conception is clear in his recognition that texts are always already multimodal, as well as his willingness to allow students to choose, experiment with, and draw upon different modes. Multimodality also came up when I asked him about his goals for his teaching. He replied,

> I think that it's important not even so much to be interacting with these specific texts but to, kind of, learn to interact with texts as a broader concept than just a book, even. Like, texts can be referring to any sort of . . . cultural phenomenon or event. Anything. So that students can kind of just learn to think critically about them. (pers. comm., February 24, 2011)

Max's idea of intertextuality, because it was so central to his conception of literacy, propelled him to an understanding of texts that included other media besides books, in addition to a recognition of books themselves as multimodal. Max also believed that all texts were connected, and in order for his idea to make sense, he had to construe texts more broadly. His teaching embraced Freire's idea of literacy as "reading the word and the reading the world" (Freire and Macedo 1987).

Max used the protests in Egypt during the spring of 2011 as a way of getting into the discussion of nonviolence and making it relevant to his students. He told me about asking students to gather as much information as they could about it and bring it into class. Max, who had a friend in Egypt at the time, showed the class her Twitter posts. He described this moment, saying,

> This was when Mubarak had sent in, um, basically, people to try
> to incite violence . . . and there was a video of one of these people
> trying to incite violence and one person trying to fight them, and
> then the whole crowd just started yelling, "Peaceful, peaceful,
> peaceful." And, um, it was in Arabic, but I thought that was really
> powerful. And she just posted it on Twitter, so I . . . used that as a
> segue into discussing the context of nonviolence. (pers. comm.,
> February 24, 2011)

Max's comments depict the teacherly identity of someone willing to use multiple media sources as texts and to devote class time to connecting these texts to social issues. Like some of the other graduate instructors (and especially Jordi in the last chapter), he used these other media sources as a "way in" to discussion about more difficult alphabetic texts. However, Max also went further in giving these other media sources a central role in the classroom and helping students become more purposeful as they chose among different modes of expression. That is, unlike Jordi, who felt she was sometimes being indulgent by letting students engage with texts in multiple modes, or Garrett or Blake, who largely saw modes beyond alphanumeric-based communication as distracting, Max invited his students into considerations of why some modes might be chosen (or privileged) above others and how academic writing can be and is multimodal, even if we might not initially see it.

Barbara: Diversity as a Resource (Threshold Concept: Writing Provides a Representation of Ideologies and Identities*)*

Inherent in many social/critical pedagogies is a strong orientation to social justice and the inherent political and ideological nature of the classroom. These pedagogies often involve an approach to teaching that treats the diverse cultural and personal experiences with which students come to the classroom as cultural capital (see Moll et al. 1992). However, research on representing race in the classroom has demonstrated the difficulty and complexity of fostering generative discussions on race. Anne Ruggles Gere, Jennifer Buehler, Christian Dallavis, and Victoria Shaw Haviland (2009), for example, describe the struggles of K–12 preservice teachers as they try to enact a culturally responsive pedagogy while negotiating their own raced consciousness and encouraging their students to confront rather than avoid race and racism in the classroom and their writing. Barbara's struggles with how to encourage students to bring their experiences to classroom discussions effectively and appropriately are further evidence of the need for support structures for new graduate instructors as they incorporate multicultural texts and encourage students to engage with discussions on race and racism.

Barbara demonstrated her commitment to highlighting racial, ethnic, and cultural diversity when I observed her second class. When I asked how she felt about the material she was teaching, Barbara replied, "Uh, the frontier issue . . . I think I probably could still rework it and add different texts that I'd feel more passionate about. You know, especially the Caucasian male perspectives, essays from the standard syllabus aren't that . . . it's just kind of bland" (pers. comm., March 3, 2011). Barbara's comments reminded me of our discussion during her interview, when she talked about wanting to be able to channel multiple voices in her own writing. She appeared to bring this idea to her teaching as well in her desire to include multiple cultural perspectives to the discussion she was having with her students about the American West.

Barbara knew that in order to invite (rather than discourage or silence) diverse perspectives, she had to encourage students from nonwhite and non-American backgrounds to speak up about these backgrounds in class. In discussing the class she was teaching in the fall, Barbara had told me she was surprised to have so many white students, especially given Public U's reputation as having a diverse student body. In the spring, Barbara was gratified to have a more culturally and linguistically diverse group. At the same time, she found this diversity was not necessarily bringing the richness to discussion she had anticipated. She told me,

Yeah, my class is a lot more diverse, this semester, you know, I have ESL students and people from different ethnicities or backgrounds. But I really want to go to one of those diversity seminars at the [center at Public for teaching and faculty development] because I still don't feel totally comfortable. Like, I was really excited about it, like, oh, they'll really have a more raucous discussion about all this material, but then they weren't doing it on their own, and I wasn't sure how to start. (pers. comm., March 3, 2011)

What Barbara was searching for was a way to make her classroom a place where her students felt comfortable drawing on these backgrounds. However, she was beginning to understand that students of all backgrounds can tend to avoid discussing issues relating to race (Durst 1999; Gere et al. 2009). She explained, "You don't want to say, 'Oh, well, you're an immigrant, how do you, you know, feel about his characterization of them?'" Barbara had the sensitivity to see that she couldn't assume her students would feel comfortable being representatives for their cultural or ethnic group. Her experiences demonstrate that culturally responsive pedagogy is difficult even for graduate instructors who don't believe in the myth of instructor neutrality. Implicit in her comments is also her struggle to negotiate her own raced identity as a white woman and how that might impact, and even silence, many of her students.

What Barbara did observe, though, was that some of these perspectives were showing up in her students' papers. She noted, "I mean I, I like that they're a lot more diverse. You know, I had an Egyptian student, and the Egyptian thing was going on, and so that student ended up writing about that in his nonviolence paper" (pers. comm., March 3, 2011). Barbara wasn't alone in these feelings: Jordi and Garrett (profiled in the last chapter) remarked that they wanted to get students talking about issues like race and social justice and for students to contribute their knowledge to these discussions.

Although these three made social/critical issues and interpretations of texts a priority, they struggled to incorporate the kind of problem-posing education that would allow students to contribute these resources in class, a sign they needed more support and guidance in enacting culturally responsive pedagogy. These challenges are understandable; coming to an understanding of one's own raced consciousness and how it might impact the classroom is, as Gere et al. (2009) argue, complex "identity work," which takes place through "gradual and halting processes by which beginning teachers work towards new understandings of their own perceptions and blind spots" (843). Further, if I'm being honest, negotiating my own raced consciousness as well as my students' continues to be a challenge, even after many years of teaching. The practicum at Public spent two weeks (out of the total of thirteen) discussing issues related to race and diversity. Although two class periods may be more than many pedagogy courses spend, it's still not enough.

Barbara's experiences also demonstrate that, in addition to threshold concepts about writing (or literacy), new graduate instructors also must grapple with threshold concepts *about teaching*. Based on her own experiences as a creative writer, and particularly her clear recognition of how other people acted as her literacy sponsors, I suspect Barbara would quickly be a convert to the threshold concept, articulated by Victor Villanueva (2015), that writing is both a reflection of and a way of discovering or even constituting our identities. Yet Barbara also struggles with how to *teach* writing in a way that acknowledges how identity, ideology, and raced consciousness shape how individuals read and write.

Research demonstrates that enacting culturally responsive pedagogies can even be difficult for more experienced instructors. In an interview with *JAC*, Ira Shor observes that many instructors "haven't seen alternative methods [to traditional, lecture-based pedagogies], . . . haven't grown up with them, . . . can't easily observe them, . . . [and] don't know what the goals are" (Buffington and Moneyhun 1997, 7). Even graduate instructors like Barbara and Max who are game for trying approaches that foreground student needs, identities, and interests and making their classrooms more collaborative might not have witnessed similar classrooms in the course of their own educations.

The practicum at Public seemed to be giving the graduate instructors support in understanding and enacting pedagogies structured around the concept of literacy as social, situated, and ideological. Barbara and Max revealed their willingness to try out multimodal teaching strategies and pedagogies that foregrounded the social nature of literacy (like small-group work and peer review), and to engage students in discussions about the ideological nature of literacy, because the assumptions undergirding these strategies matched their prior conceptions of literacy. But becoming a teacher is a long-term process and enacting these kinds of pedagogies is difficult. For too many graduate instructors whose fields are outside composition, the initially difficult and counterintuitive nature of the threshold concepts of writing and teaching, as well as a lack of continued support beyond their formal pedagogy education, might make them abandon these views and the teaching that stems from them.

The danger is that we will deemphasize or ignore the issues instructors like Barbara and Max are having because, as Grutsch McKinney and Chiseri-Strater (2003) say, they are "telling our story—composition is important and I love it" (69). To put it another way, the fact that Max and Barbara were excited about the practicum readings, seemed to understand them, and were attempting to enact them in the classroom didn't mean they weren't still in need of support or that they wouldn't need to continue to learn about composition pedagogy beyond the first semester. Moreover, seeing graduate instructors' views through the conceptions-of-literacy framework reminds us that even social/critical literacy views are ideological; they direct our attention to some aspects of the literacy experience while obscuring others.

IMPLICATIONS OF THRESHOLD CONCEPTS
FOR TEACHER EDUCATION

While the current study wasn't designed with the threshold concepts in mind, my in-depth look at conceptions of literacy suggests the role prior views and experiences might play as new graduate instructors come into contact with threshold concepts. That is, these graduate instructors entered their graduate coursework and their teaching classrooms already having crossed a number of thresholds they may not even have realized they had crossed. Whereas some graduate instructors, like Barbara and Max, had already crossed thresholds that gave them footholds in the new territory of composition pedagogy, others found the portals into this pedagogy more difficult to navigate.

In a recent piece in *Inside Higher Ed*, John Warner (2018) describes his experience of discovering *Naming What We Know*, stating, "In many cases, I realized I did indeed *know* this thing, but didn't know I knew it until it was expressed so clearly and so well by an expert." Although he frequently blogs and writes about writing, Warner (like the participants in this chapter) is more a creative writer than a compositionist, as his acknowledgement of the authors in *Naming* as experts, rather than himself, indicates. But Warner's description of his experience is still telling—that he wants to champion the book because the concepts he read already made sense to him; like Jordi and Max, he already *knew* them, even if he wasn't able to articulate them. This description speaks, I think, to both the value and the limitations of the threshold concepts. For someone like Warner, who already knows something about writing and pedagogy, having access to the concepts and, perhaps, reading them "piecemeal" so "each concept gets sufficient time to roll around" in their head may well be useful (Warner 2018).

In terms of *Naming*'s value for compositionists, I also like the feminist connotations of the project of *naming*, as it evokes the political practice of naming both what we as feminists (or compositionists) see and the problems that don't yet have a name (see Friedan 2001). As Adler-Kassner and Wardle (2015) state in *Naming* and elsewhere, being able to put a label on what we know can have tremendous power for us in asserting our expertise. Indeed, the criticisms of *Naming* I note at the beginning of this chapter, and particularly the view that *Naming* may only point to a narrow version of the field rather than representing it in its complexity, may well also support *Naming's* importance in negotiating some of the marginalization many compositionists are experiencing within the discipline. That is, seeing the fissures, as well as what, and who, gets championed, can be telling as we reconsider what it means to be part of this discipline and what aspects of the discipline are unfortunately being marginalized.

The case studies presented in this chapter also point to some of the potential limitations of *Naming*, as they demonstrate that even graduate instructors whose ideas might appear to be in line with the threshold concepts bring their disciplinary perspectives to their understanding of the concepts. The four threshold concepts I identify as representative of Barbara's and Max's views also happen to be ones that illustrate fundamental aspects of creative writing. The concept of literacy as social makes sense for individuals who have experiences in creative writing workshops, which acknowledge the interactional nature of writing. In addition, the two concepts having to do with textuality, intertextuality and multimodality, are not the province of composition studies alone. As Bazerman (2004) argues, the term *intertextuality* was coined by Julia Kristeva (1980) and is often more associated with literary studies than with composition. And, as Bazerman further shows, the literary definition of intertextuality, which is more concerned with "the status of the author and the modes of consciousness expressed in fiction," may be insufficient for composition instructors who need knowledge of how to help students recognize and deploy various kinds of intertextual references and see how different disciplines and genres both allow for and constrain the types of explicit and implicit intertextual references writers can make (59).

Multimodality too can be considered an interdisciplinary concept, and it is one receiving much attention in creative writing, which is experimenting with what it means to create content that can be molded and used across a number of different platforms and that engages with multiple modes (see Goldsmith 2008). Because of these differing disciplinary lenses, new graduate instructors may well also see some threshold concepts as representing their views, even as they interpret the concepts differently from how compositionists would. This difference can be both positive and negative; as Kimberly Costino and Sunny Hyon (2011) argue, concepts like genre, which have been theorized in multiple fields, can act as disciplinary bridges and encourage interdisciplinary collaboration; however, such bridges are only productive if those on either side also articulate their unspoken assumptions about terms they use as shorthand.

Related to the problems that can be caused by assumptions is that although the threshold concepts are delivered in ways that suggest their authors are naming and describing them for newcomers, in their effort to condense the concepts down to their essence, some may not be sufficiently elaborated for novices. Also telling is that some of the concepts make intertextual references only insiders (or relative insiders) to composition theory would get. For example, in his chapter "Writing Is a Social and Rhetorical Activity," Roozen (2015b) references "the available means of persuasion we take up when we write" without explicitly referencing Aristotle or stating that this is a concept from rhetorical theory (18). While a novice without a basic background in rhetoric may be able to understand the sentence containing this reference, an insider who has read Aristotle will likely get more out of it. This example leads to the question of what newcomers may need to know *before* being able to understand the threshold concepts.

To put it in terms of the graduate practicum, we can't just assign new graduate instructors the threshold concepts and expect them to understand and apply them in their teaching. Because threshold concepts are conceptually difficult and counterintuitive, only more seasoned members of the discipline are likely to fully understand them. To put it another way, the threshold concepts in *Naming* aren't for undergraduates, and they're not really for new graduate students either: they're for us, by which I mean more experienced, seasoned members of the field. This is not to say threshold concepts don't have value for novices; I have presented upper-level undergraduates with threshold concepts *as a concept* (i.e., that they are counterintuitive and act as "portals" into a discipline) and have asked them to come up with their own concepts before introducing them to one or two from *Naming*. Usually, the ones I present have either already been articulated in different ways in readings the students have done prior in the course or are ones we will expand on and engage with in other ways. The key is that graduate instructors must be interacting with and coming up with their own concepts for them to have meaning.

Chris Anson (2015) also notes the importance of approach in incorporating threshold concepts into teacher education, stating "certain threshold concepts introduced too glibly can trigger false assumptions, resistance, or confusion among faculty" (216). Anson's assertion recalls Welch's (1993) and others' arguments against the practicum as a site of "conversion" and the potential for real harm if practica instructors and mentors appear to be forcing graduate instructors to adopt a particular view that runs counter to their conceptions of literacy. That is, the "resistance" noted again and again in the research on graduate-instructor education may be more revealing of our failure to engage newcomers' conceptions of literacy and the funds of knowledge they bring to their teaching.

CONCLUSION: CONCEPTIONS OF LITERACY AND DISCIPLINARITY

Anne Ruggles Gere, Sarah Swofford, Naomi Silver, and Melody Pugh's (2015) concepts of discipline and disciplinarity may help shed light on the tension between, on the one hand, asserting our field's knowledge (especially in sites like the composition practicum), and, on the other, accounting for the fact that there are also things about writing and literacy we don't know and that graduate instructors come to us already knowing, having already crossed a number of thresholds. Gere et al. (2015) argue that *disciplines* "are traditionally characterized by a degree of *insularity, and even stasis,* in which . . . knowledge remains bound and stable" (244; emphasis mine). Disciplines are thus "*bordered and relatively fixed* because they have 'as their primary and privileged referent the discipline itself'" (Marcovich and Shinn quoted in Gere et al. 2005, 244; emphasis mine). Instead of this limiting conception of *discipline*, Gere et al. instead propose the concept of *disciplinarity*, in which disciplines become more "flexible entities," allowing stakeholders to "participate in activities or projects that bring together different combinations of disciplinary representatives" (245). Disciplinarity thus entails "borderland interactions" that call upon resources and representatives from different combinations of disciplines (245). An example of disciplinarity would be asking graduate instructors with backgrounds in creative writing to bring in their knowledge of writing workshops, or their conceptions of intertextuality or multimodality, and putting them into productive tension with some of the concepts from *Naming*.

Certainly there are instances in which compositionists may want the borders of our discipline to be less permeable. For instance, as I contend at the beginning of this chapter, in the context of being recognized as writing experts in our larger institutions or making hiring decisions about composition, we might adopt a more rhetorical approach to our disciplinarity and strategically position composition as a bordered discipline. Moreover, in arguing for a longer, more robust minimal preparation for composition teachers, we should emphasize the decades of expertise we have developed in writing, while simultaneously building interdisciplinary bridges through shared values with colleagues in our and other departments.

If we acknowledge composition practica as some of the spaces in which "borderland interactions" happen, we might begin to see them as opportunities to put different disciplinary and ingrained cultural ways of valuing literacy into dialogue with each other. Indeed, the term *borderland interactions* could easily describe many of the experiences detailed in this book. Acknowledging the insights and perspectives new graduate instructors bring with them also helps keep us honest as we advocate for certain pedagogical approaches above others (see Ede 2004). Moreover, thinking of the practicum in terms of disciplinarity acknowledges more fully some of the central realities of our field, including the crucial fact that writing (and literacy) are the business of all disciplines.

The education of new graduate instructors reveals perhaps most poignantly the complexities of being writing and literacy experts and of how composition courses get staffed; as one reviewer of this book put it, the fact that graduate students in literary studies and creative writing teach these courses makes first-year writing much more complicated than other introductory courses. However, if the insights of literacy studies have taught us anything, it should be the harm of constructing ourselves as gatekeepers. Thus, as Ede (2004) argues, quoting Karen Paley, we must avoid the binary extremes of either "'disciplinary terrorism,' where the effort to argue for one paradigm requires the demolition" of other paradigms *or* renouncing our claim that we are a discipline (77). Instead, I think we can, in sites like the practicum, assert composition's disciplinary knowledge while acknowledging how graduate instructors' conceptions of literacy complicate or reveal the "troublesome" nature of this knowledge.

To that end, I argue, along with Goldblatt (2017), that we must return to some of the concepts from literacy studies that undergird composition pedagogies but that have unfortunately felt marginalized within composition in recent years, in collections like *Naming* and elsewhere. Acknowledging, for example, that writing is just one aspect of literacy can help new graduate instructors see how their experiences beyond those with academic writing influence how they conceptualize writing and teaching (and, indeed, the ways historical conceptions of literacy have undergirded how we imagine the first-year course). In the next and final chapter, I discuss how we can draw further on the insights of literacy studies to rethink the education of new graduate instructors.

5

CONCLUSION

An Emphasis on Literacy in the Practicum Course

*Students come to the classroom with preconceptions about how
the world works. If their initial understanding is not engaged,
they may fail to grasp the new concepts and information that
are taught, or they may learn them for purposes of a test but
revert to their preconceptions outside of the classroom.*
—John D. Bransford, James W. Pellegrino,
and M. Suzanne Donovan

In the fall of 2017, seven years after I began my study, I am on
the phone interviewing Lily. It's an auspicious occasion: the
next day she will defend her doctoral dissertation exploring
how to extract writing principles from yoga. As I talk to Lily,
my daughter in my lap, Lily's daughter, just under a year old,
fusses in the background, and I realize how much has changed
since we first sat down together after the second meeting of the
practicum at Public.

Although a half-hour interview, punctuated in bursts by a
three-year-old and a ten-month-old, cannot give a full picture
of everything that has changed for Lily, it does offer a glimpse
into how her conception of literacy has evolved beyond that first
semester and year. Lily has read portions of this manuscript, and
we begin talking about whether she still sees literacy in largely
individual, spiritual ways. Lily responds,

> I'm back to that [expressive, personal views of literacy] a little
> more than I was . . . minus the part about where there's a core
> author that needs to be released. I don't know if I ever believed
> in that, or I guess maybe I did but mostly in relationship to
> artistic stuff and theater. I think I'm back though in some ways

DOI: 10.7330/9781607329343.c005

[to more personal, spiritual understandings of literacy]. I read Freire and that changed my perspective a lot. (pers. comm., September 26, 2017)

As we talk, it becomes clear that while Lily's views are still inspired by her backgrounds in yoga and acting, they have also changed. She tells me Freire's concept of critical consciousness, which she read about in the spring of 2011, not long after our final interview, changed her way of viewing individual agency. She also took courses in disability studies and the history of rhetoric that made her think more about discourse's role in oppression. As she talks, I point out to Lily that even much of her language as changed—instead of authenticity or integrity, she's talking about agency and the Other.

I ask Lily if the principles of the Kripalu, aligning what you think, what you feel, what you say, and what you do, are still important to her. She laughs. "Yeah, that's so funny," she replies. "I haven't thought about the Kripalu in a long time. I guess I'm much more focused on the concept of agency." Lily continues, though, to say that the concept of agency does relate to the Kripalu. But clearly, her studies over the past seven years have also enriched and complicated her thinking.

Lily tells me her turn back to personal ways of thinking about literacy occurred partly because she's been isolated for so long with her dissertation. She also describes her sense of helplessness (to return to the concept of agency) now that Donald Trump is the president and shares that she's teaching a 5-5 load at a nearby professional college. Lily states,

I feel guilty saying that because I feel like Trump is supposed to make us feel like, fierce, like we need to do something. But, I also, where I'm teaching right now, I just feel like the students are less engaged, and so that makes it harder to think about activist principles and how they might relate to teaching.

In short, Lily's learning trajectory is fueled by a number of influences—her frustration that she is writing about yoga and agency but can't get her students to care, her feelings of helplessness in the face of a Trump presidency, and the huge burden of a 5-5 teaching load. Her words, again, suggest that even people in the quintessentially most academic of all academic programs—the doctoral program—bring with them multiple experiences, many nonacademic, that shape their concepts of literacy, writing, and teaching. And clearly, these experiences continue to shape them, even as they are exposed to new perspectives on literacy. It's evident that Lily is not exactly the same person I spoke to seven years ago. *But* she also *is* the same person I spoke to seven years ago.

My interview with Lily points to several strands that have appeared throughout this book and that I want to reconsider in this final chapter. Most immediately, and as the epigraph for this chapter points out, Lily's statements highlight the complexity and power of conceptions of literacy. We cannot understand someone's conception just by asking them about their writing or about a favorite teacher; although these sponsors and experiences are significant, other unexpected influences on our literacy development, like yoga, a grandparent's occupation, or a favorite musical artist can hold equal sway and be more explanatory than typically "academic" literacies and experiences.

Moreover, conceptions of literacy, like identities, are both *dynamic* and *fixed*. They are dynamic in that they change in their focus and resonance across time and contexts. They are fixed in that certain experiences are still defining for us, even as they gain richness or resonate differently according to new experiences. As Taczak puts it in her description of her own graduate-school experience, "The experienced curriculum does not follow a 'straight line' but rather follows a recursive path— 'doubling back on itself, leaping forward, and, at times, grinding to a halt'" (Lay quoted in Taczak and Yancey 2015, 149). At this, the very latest point in her graduate-school career, Lily's conception of literacy is still very personal and spiritual and influenced by Eastern yoga philosophy. However, reading Freire and others also made Lily look back on and evaluate these experiences differently, what Donna Qualley (2016), following David Perkins and Gavriel Salomon (1988), describes as "backward-reaching" transfer, in which individuals come to a "retrospective understanding" of prior experiences (94). Lily's experiences point to the importance of handling new graduate instructors' past experiences with care, while also giving them opportunities to denaturalize these experiences, putting them into productive tension and dialogue with composition pedagogy.

I began the study informing this book with an examination of theories of literacy. Literacy, I hoped, would be more expansive and informative than theoretical frameworks that examine only new graduate instructors' resistance or their attitudes toward writing (see Dryer 2012; Ebest 2005; Farris 1996; Reid 2009; Reid, Estrem, and Belcheir 2012). Throughout this book, I've considered the following questions: What does it mean to be a new graduate instructor who thinks of literacy in the ways I've described? What strengths and obstacles do these conceptions bring? In this final chapter, I want to (re)consider two more questions: What does it mean to be a writing program administrator (or mentor or practica instructor) who knows or suspects that their graduate instructors think in these ways? More broadly, what does it mean for the discipline of composition that we have many new graduate instructors (and faculty members) who think of literacy in these terms?

As this last question implies, the issue of disciplinarity is essential to our understanding of graduate instructors' early experiences with teaching and composition pedagogy. Although many graduate instructors see themselves as composition scholars and will, like Karen and Lily, have the continuing opportunity to see and resee their conceptions of literacy through the lens of other perspectives communicated to them in scholarship, conferences, mentoring, and so forth, more graduate instructors, because of time and disciplinary affiliation, will not have formal opportunities to continue this development. And we know continued support is crucial as graduate instructors continue the long, developmental process of becoming teachers. While I argue for the importance of conceptions of literacy, rather than disciplinarity, as a determining factor in how graduate instructors teach and see themselves as teachers, the preceding chapters demonstrate that disciplinary identity overlaps in some ways with literacy conceptions. In addition, new graduate instructors' disciplines and programs of study often either enable them to revisit what they weren't ready to learn, or, perhaps more commonly, communicate to them that they have already learned what they needed to in a single-semester, one-shot course. Finally, as I discuss in the last chapter, practica instructors' senses of their own disciplinarity and those of their graduate students can influence our view of the graduate instructors we educate in practica courses, for better or worse.

Reid (2007) says of her experience of reading a collection meant for beginning teachers, "I discovered . . . ideas that I probably should have learned in the previous decade but hadn't—in part because *I wasn't ready to learn them earlier*" (247; emphasis mine). New graduate instructors' conceptions of literacy position them as "ready to learn" some ideas about composition but not others. They determine, in part, what they are willing to engage with and entertain and what they leave aside. The stories of new graduate instructors I have told here show we cannot ignore or dismiss new graduate instructors' conceptions of literacy. Instead, we must, as Restaino (2012) argues, "honor beginnings" (119). Following Restaino, I think those of us who educate graduate instructors or new composition faculty must think more deeply about what it means to respect the positions they bring with them to this education and understand these positions are informed by a long history of literacy sponsors and experiences.

I begin by revisiting the claim made throughout this book: that graduate instructors come to their practica with powerful (but often tacit) preconceptions of what literacy is and should be and that these attitudes affect the way they teach their composition courses. In order to examine this claim from another angle, I use some of the methods of analysis described in Estrem and Reid's (2012) study in order to contextualize the influence of graduate instructors' conceptions of literacy amidst other potential influences. I then outline some recommendations for practicum courses to best support graduate instructors as they begin the process of considering and reconciling best practices for composition teaching with their preexisting (and sometimes changing) views of literacy.

INFLUENCES ON NEW GRADUATE
INSTRUCTORS' TEACHING

The overarching argument of this book points to the strong influence of graduate instructors' conceptions of literacy on their pedagogy and attitudes toward literacy. Although the practicum appeared to have some sway over their beliefs, because of the short time of the semester and the compelling nature of previous conceptions, its influence was filtered through graduate instructors' preexisting beliefs. Throughout this book, I have used descriptions of how graduate instructors' conceptions changed—or didn't—over the course of their first semester of teaching to make this case.

I model the following analysis on Estrem and Reid's (2012) attempt to categorize and track the "combination of beliefs . . . [graduate instructors] hold prior to teaching as well as the impact of composition teaching principles" (458). To do this, Estrem and Reid's (2012) research assistants interviewed twenty-nine graduate instructors across two sites over a period of three years. In the interview protocol, the graduate instructors were asked two key questions: "What do you see as three to four key principles for your teaching or tutoring of writing?" and "Could you say where those beliefs come from?" (454). The researchers categorized the answers to the second question, which was designed to get at principles or beliefs about teaching writing as derived from the following:

1. Formal study, including composition scholarship

2. Personal experience, belief, family values, or intuition

3. Experience teaching or tutoring

4. The community of peers and mentors within which they work (458)

I approached a similar research question, one about where the ideas and beliefs informing the graduate instructors' teaching were coming from, in a slightly different way. As I describe in chapter 1, I interviewed each of the graduate instructors three times; once as an initial interview to find about their backgrounds and conceptions of literacy and twice following visits to each of their classrooms. Consequently, two of the interviews were more embedded than Estrem and Reid's (2012) in that they took place in the specific context of asking graduate instructors about the teaching practices I had just observed. In our interviews, I repeated back to the graduate instructors the activities and practices I had witnessed and then asked them about how they decided to include each activity and what their learning goals were. I asked this question in different ways depending on the context and how much detail the graduate instructors gave in describing their thinking and planning process. Most often my question was, Where did the idea for [name of teaching strategy/activity I witnessed] come from?

I divided my coding categories up more than Estrem and Reid (2012) did to account for the multiple influences the graduate instructors cited as they talked about their teaching. Specifically, I used the following categories:

1. Curriculum or standard syllabus for College Composition

2. Peers or FYC community

3. Other grad program, including ideas communicated to the graduate instructors in other seminar classes or formal graduate education before they enrolled at Public

4. Practicum, including readings, the practicum professor, or ideas communicated during class meetings

5. Experience as a student

6. Teaching experience, including past teaching experiences and ongoing experiences teaching College Composition

7. Personal experience, belief, or intuition

I coded a total of two hundred content units in which the seven focal participants described influences on their teaching. In the graph in figure 5.1, I show how the numbers for each of the seven coding categories above were distributed.[1]

These findings suggest the graduate instructors in this study drew overwhelmingly on personal experiences, beliefs, or intuition about literacy in deciding how to teach their composition classes. I should note that although I see conceptions of literacy and personal beliefs as overlapping categories, graduate

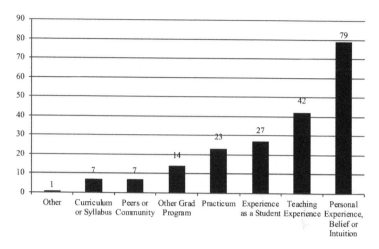

Figure 5.1. Influence on teaching

instructors also held beliefs that didn't seem linked to conceptions of literacy (at least in any apparent way). In the next section, I give more context for how the graduate instructors responded to these questions.

1. Curriculum or Standard Syllabus for College Composition

The responses in this category indicated that the graduate instructors were doing something because they were "supposed to" or because it was mandated by the curriculum for College Composition or the syllabus. For example, Jordi said she was teaching synthesis as "referring to three sources in a paragraph" not because it was something she valued or had done in her own education but because the assignment mandated it. When I asked her about where the idea for having three sources per paragraph came from, she responded, "Whoever wrote the prompt" (pers. comm., November 18, 2010). This response is telling because it shows how graduate instructors can become dislocated from assignments and other teaching materials they have not had a hand in designing, which has the unfortunate effect of making them feel as though they are just going through the motions and teaching something conceived by someone else.[2]

2. Peers or FYC Community

Barbara referred most often to using other graduate instructors as a resource. In particular, she and Karen developed a mentoring relationship that lasted beyond the first semester. Estrem and Reid (2012) separate this category from what they refer to as "formal instruction" in pedagogy, including the practicum, because they see it as a different kind of interaction. In particular, they note that "while TAs do turn to peer mentors for practical help, they have less frequent theorized or reflective conversations with peers" (461). However, in Barbara's descriptions, her collaborations with Karen seemed much more reflective and theorized. That is, Karen helped Barbara move beyond centering her classes just on reading and discussion to make them into writing workshops where students practiced skills like counterarguments, using formats like blog posts in order to get a sense of writing as responding to others. Karen also reinforced for Barbara the importance of scaffolding and sequencing tasks in these courses. However, six of the seven content units I coded came from Barbara's data (Jordi also mentioned getting ideas from Garrett for her classes), suggesting peer influence was not as important as other influences for the other graduate instructors or at least that it didn't occur to the graduate instructors to mention these interactions.

3. Other Grad Program

Although Estrem and Reid (2012) put all "formal instruction" into one category, graduate instructors' mentions of influences from past graduate programs or even from other seminar professors or graduate-school experiences appeared, in this study, to be distinct from the influences of the practicum. Especially since I wanted to focus on how much influence the practicum has, I saw it as significant that whereas Lily, for example, mentioned theorists to justify her pedagogy, these theorists were never ones she had read in the practicum. For example, Lily mentioned "transmission of knowledge versus knowledge-making," which she had read about for her master's degree in English education (pers. comm., November 15, 2010). She also discussed the theories of Lucy Calkins and Louise Rosenblatt. In addition, Barbara described how fiction workshops, in which you "always have to say why" something was working or not working, helped her give better feedback on student papers (pers. comm., October 22, 2010).

These comments indicate that graduate instructors are influenced, as Dryer (2012) says, by transfer from "other system[s]," including creative writing workshops and literature seminars they are currently experiencing or have experienced recently (443). Because new graduate instructors rely on experiences that extend well beyond the practicum course to inform their pedagogy, it is crucial that WPAs have discussions with their colleagues across the graduate programs their graduate instructors come from in order to create consistent cultures of writing pedagogy.

4. Practicum

The influence of the practicum, as I have suggested, was not neutral. Not surprisingly, the graduate instructors who mentioned it the most were Jordi, Karen, and Barbara, who were the ones who drew on their peers as resources and generally appeared the most committed to learning from the practicum. They were also the graduate instructors who gave the impression of spending the most time developing their own activities for classes. For example, in the following excerpt, Jordi refers to the double-entry journal technique created by Ann Berthoff, which is described in *The St. Martin's Guide to Teaching Writing* (Glenn and Goldthwaite 2008, 240).

> Um, I remembered the two-panel thing that's been mentioned in a lot of the . . . articles [David assigned], or, I guess in that thing we use? *St. Martin's?* (pers. comm., November 18, 2010)

I quote this passage because it demonstrates the difficulty for the graduate instructors of calling to mind the specific ways the practicum influenced their teaching. Jordi begins by calling the double-entry technique the "two-panel thing" before misidentifying where it came from and then finally remembering the original source of the activity. I discuss some potential reasons for (and implications of) this difficulty at the end of this section.

Karen mentioned using the work of John Dewey, which she read for another class she took with David the following spring semester (the semester of our second interview), to create and revise some of her lesson plans for CC. Although her exposure to Dewey wasn't from the practicum, I mention it here because it suggests the possibility for graduate instructors to draw on theorists like Dewey in their practice. However, it also seems as if graduate instructors are more apt to draw on theories of composition in subsequent semesters, suggesting that while, as Restaino (2012) argues, reflection may be difficult during graduate instructors' hectic first semesters, it can emerge later on with appropriate support (24).

It also seems as if there might have been a gendered component in that the men, Blake, Garrett and Max, rarely mentioned the practicum when talking about their teaching decisions. I was especially surprised at how little Max mentioned it, given how much his conception of literacy appeared to align with ideas mentioned in the practicum. However, given the difficulty of calling to mind the specific influences of the practicum, I argue at the end of this section that it might just be that much of the learning that results from the graduate practicum is invisible.

5. Experience as a Student

Many of the graduate instructors mentioned teachers they viewed as models for the kind of teacher they wanted to be. For example, Max discussed a literature professor from his undergraduate education, saying she "really tried to take a back seat in the classroom and would try to let students discuss texts on their own and did a lot with peer reviewing as well" (pers. comm., October 25, 2010). Max used this professor as a model for his "guide-on-the-side" approach in his own classroom, which seemed to work well in conjunction with what he was learning in the practicum, although, as I note, he never mentioned the practicum directly as an influence. As I discuss in the previous chapter, Blake in particular was also influenced significantly by a teacher he had as an undergraduate. While we should encourage graduate instructors to identify teachers who were influential for them, a nod to the apprenticeship of observation they have been participating in for the greater part of their lives, as Blake's experience demonstrates, modeling their teaching after these influences can be limiting, even as it might give graduate instructors confidence or a benchmark to strive for. In particular, negative views like the one Blake's college writing instructor had of undergraduate writing could be damaging if practica instructors do not provide ways for graduate instructors to intervene in them.

6. Teaching Experience

The graduate instructors drew heavily on their teaching experience in their descriptions of influences on their pedagogy. Although this influence might seem obvious for Karen, who had the most prior experience teaching, or even Lily, who had a master's degree in English education along with some prior experience, it also appeared among even the inexperienced graduate instructors, suggesting they were drawing upon their experiences as new teachers in an ongoing way. Estrem and Reid (2012) also note that "new teachers' observations of their own students prevail over data and theories about writing and learning" (462). The comments I coded for this influence often seemed to communicate ideas like, "I did this last time and it worked (or didn't work)." For example,

> It was just something I used last semester. I guess to try and diversify the group work and make it so that they were engaged with each other because I, you know, one of the [examples of] student feedback I got was to vary the group work, so that every

group isn't presenting on the same thing. (Barbara, pers. comm., March 3, 2010)

This semester is definitely better because I have some idea of what I'm doing. You know, I know that certain things didn't work, and I changed them. I have some clue to how they're going to respond and am prepared to deal with that more, I guess. (Jordi, pers. comm., March 14, 2011)

Although both these excerpts come from interviews with graduate instructors in their second semester of teaching, the graduate instructors mentioned their teaching experiences in the first semester as well, discussing in particular how they modified approaches when lessons went particularly well or poorly. Teaching has, to quote Ede (2004), such "an in-your-face immediacy" that it makes sense that new graduate instructors would ground their decisions in their ongoing successes and disappointments in the classroom (148). As with their experiences as students, practica instructors should encourage graduate instructors to draw on their experiences as teachers *if* they can be critical and reflective about why something worked or didn't work. However, too often graduate instructors can discard an activity that didn't go well when some minor changes to the activity would suffice. For example, I often mentor novice instructors who have lost their faith in peer review because it didn't go well a few times, not realizing effective peer review must be modeled and targeted so students are focusing on giving feedback only on certain aspects of the writing. Some minor adjustments (showing a video about peer review or having discussions about students' past experiences with peer review) before a peer review begins can easily turn it into a more productive activity. Mentors and practica instructors should continually ask graduate instructors to reflect upon activities that work or don't work and provide feedback on these reflections.

7. Personal Experience, Belief, or Intuition

The graduate instructors mentioned personal experience, belief, or intuition as the source for most of their teaching decisions. At some points, they described this more, locating it in a particular idea they had about writing, while at others they just said something like "That's just what I think" or "I think it works."

> I started doing it [collecting journal responses] at the beginning because I thought that it would be a way for them to feel like somebody was reading it. There was a point; somebody was reading it. (Lily, pers. comm., November 15, 2010)

> I mean, it [using "I"] distracts you from what's at hand. Unless you're writing about your parents or something like that, you know, what business do you have in the conversation? . . . You know, and you do have business in there, of course, but I mean, you have to know the proper place. . . . So, anyway, that's my perspective. (Garrett, pers. comm., October 20, 2010)

> It's going to become dry and boring, and should academic writing be dry and boring? Well, no. I don't think so, and that's part of my own little personal agenda [*laughs*]. But, I mean, I do believe this. (Karen, pers. comm., March 4, 2011)

Estrem and Reid's (2012) study found similarly that personal experiences, beliefs, and intuition figured strongly in graduate instructors' responses, but their results were more evenly distributed between the category of "Personal Experience, Belief, or Intuition" and what they call "Formal Study," which included one-semester practica courses. However, Estrem and Reid (2012) also conducted a second analysis that looked at *only the initial responses* the graduate instructors gave. The results of this analysis matched mine more in that the graduate instructors often began by naming either their personal experiences or their teaching experiences and then, after pausing to consider further, adding something like "the readings too, but I can't say which one" (459). In other words, they noted that personal and teaching experiences seemed to come more quickly to mind for the graduate instructors. In my study, perhaps because of the context or the way I asked the question, the graduate instructors did not mention the practicum course as much, even as an afterthought, as they did in Estrem and Reid's study. However, both studies still point to the strong influence of graduate instructors' conceptions of literacy.

I also noticed another pattern in the graduate instructors' responses, which was that sometimes they did not mention the practicum as an influence *even when I knew they were drawing directly upon something they had learned in the practicum.* For example, both Lily and Barbara used an activity they learned from the practicum in which the graduate instructors asked students to pick pivotal scenes from *Kindred* and act them out. But when I asked them about how they decided to do this activity, neither of them acknowledged it was modeled on something they had seen in the practicum. In addition, Lily's practice of collecting journal responses was something David had suggested during a practicum session and that is described in the *The St. Martin's Guide to Teaching Writing,* which she read for the practicum (see Glenn and Goldthwaite 2008, 166–67). But in the interview excerpt I quote above, she attributes it to something she had decided to do because it was in accordance with her beliefs and made sense to her.

On the one hand, graduate instructors' tendency to not mention the practicum suggests the power of their literacy conceptions. That is, they were willing to use ideas and practices from the practicum but only once they could justify them based on understandings of literacy they already had. To put it another way, activities and theories from the practicum only become useful and useable once graduate instructors have found ways for them to fit with their conceptions of literacy. I am reminded here of Dewey's (1944) idea that we cannot hand ideas to students as if they were bricks (4); in order to learn, the graduate instructors had to interact with and transform the knowledge they gained from the practicum and other formal and informal sources.

On the other hand, the graduate instructors' tendency to not mention the practicum's influence also suggests that recent work in the area of graduate-teacher education may be underestimating its impact (see Dryer 2012; Estrem and Reid 2012; Restaino 2012). Scholarship's tendency to underestimate the practicum's influence reflects Schieber's (2016) finding that students' learning can be invisible to both themselves and their teachers (466). To be clear, I still would not go so far as to suggest, as Dobrin (2005) does, that the practicum is a "powerful mechanism" in purveying "composition's cultural capital" (6). As I have stated throughout this book, the power of the practicum in the face of graduate instructors' own theories of literacy is limited. However, I also think practica can be sites where instructors can invite graduate instructors into a process whereby they begin to identify and reconsider previous beliefs about literacy and provide the space for learning that will solidify in subsequent semesters. In the next section, I offer suggestions for how practica instructors can facilitate this learning.

RETHINKING THE GRADUATE PRACTICUM: AN EMPHASIS ON LITERACY

In the practicum syllabus and in the first week of class, David announced that the theme of the practicum course would be conceptions of literacy. In the syllabus, he clarifies this emphasis, stating,

> The purpose of this course is NOT to introduce you to the field of composition/rhetoric or to plunge you into academic debates on written language acquisition, but we do want to give you some experience with the fundamental concerns writing teachers return to again and again. The required reading should give you some orientation to wider questions while speaking to your day-to-day teaching experience. We hope to encourage a habit of praxis in teachers: a dynamic combination of theory and practice in which reflection is challenged by action and action is informed by an unfolding vision of what reading and writing can be. Often teachers are limited by what they think their students are capable of doing and what they understand literacy to be. Students can reach amazing new places if they are challenged effectively, and literacy is a far more encompassing human activity than most people recognize. This class is theoretical in that we are constantly stepping back to ask WHY, but it is practical in that we are constantly stepping forward to ask HOW. For this reason, each class session will have at least one activity designed to familiarize you with an aspect of classroom management or practice essential to moving students through the College Composition syllabus. (David, "Practicum Syllabus")

This description illuminates a number of tensions inherent in designing a practica course, including (1) the balance between theory and practice, (2) whether and how much the course should be introducing graduate instructors to the field of composition and rhetoric, and, fundamentally, (3) how we select from among all compositionists know—and need to know—and package it into a meaningful course graduate instructors can navigate amidst the demands of their other classes and an arduous teaching schedule.

These are crucial questions that have been revisited again and again throughout the history of scholarship on teacher education in composition (see especially Dobrin 2005; Fedukovich and Hall 2016; Guerra and Bawarshi 2005; Restaino 2012). However, what the syllabus description above also reveals is that *literacy*, and specifically conceptions of literacy, is central to these concerns. While practical instruction in how to manage classrooms and create lessons to scaffold literacy skills is essential, graduate instructors need to have a sense, even if it is only an emerging one, of *why* they are doing what they are doing, one that goes beyond the requirements communicated by the curriculum (which always has, at its core, assumptions about what literacy can and should accomplish). And although the course should not, as David indicates, be an introduction to composition and rhetoric, graduate instructors need a sense of the field's history—why the first courses were created at Harvard, the process movement, the social turn, and so forth—in order to develop a sense of where their own preexisting views about literacy fit within (or even complicate or contrast) some of the assumptions that undergird composition pedagogies today.

The final of the three considerations I describe above, how to choose among the many concepts that can be addressed within the truncated period of a fifteen-week course, is perhaps the most difficult and frustrating. Without claiming it to be a cure-all for institutional cultures and insufficiencies that mandate graduate teacher education take place over such an inadequately brief period, I suggest that incorporating readings and assignments that foreground literacy is one way of making already-existing tensions among graduate instructors' conceptions of literacy, personal experience and intuition, and disciplinarity more productive as they navigate their first semester and year.

One way the practicum course described here tackled this was through the Assignment-Ranking Activity (see appendix C). Designed as a data-collection tool, this activity occasioned talk among the graduate instructors about what literacy practices and goals for FYC they valued. For example, Jordi's written response to the activity is as follows:

> These rankings reflect my somewhat tenuous belief in the important of the text. . . . While I value the concept of relating text to self and text to world, I think establishing such relationships is difficult or superficial without first establishing a deep understanding of the text itself. For this reason, I've ranked assignments that center on the ideas in the text before asking students to relate those ideas to the space outside the text.

The value of this activity is that it helped graduate instructors grapple with their tacit and still-emerging beliefs about literacy. Jordi's belief in the importance of texts impacted almost everything she said in her interviews. It also was recorded in her literacy narratives, and it affected the decisions she made on a day-to-day basis in the classroom. But in some ways, she wasn't aware of just how important texts were to her or that students could interpret their work in the composition classroom differently than she did. In this passage, Jordi interprets her belief as "tenuous," a descriptor that I think both underestimates how much this belief has shaped her and also communicates that the tensions among her disciplinary identity, her conception of literacy, her sense of self, and what she felt she was required to do as a composition instructor were, in this moment, very real and pressing for her. That is, I think the word "tenuous" is indicative that something had happened during the semester that was challenging beliefs she had long held but was only beginning to articulate.

The key assignment in this literacy studies-based curriculum was the autobiographical literacy narrative assignment, which is described in the practicum syllabus as follows:

Following the theme of conceptions of literacy, I'll ask you to write a brief literacy narrative for the September 10 class and a longer literacy reflection paper due on the last day of class. In the shorter narrative (3–5 pages), please detail an experience, an interaction with another person, or a memory that is emblematic for you of your attitude toward reading and writing. This first paper will serve as a starting point for your contemplation of literacy as a force or a phenomenon in your life. I will not grade this paper but I will respond to it extensively, noting possible themes to explore. I'd like you to return to the topic in your longer reflection paper (7–10 pages), and be sure to consider BOTH reading and writing as you come to a more articulated understanding of what literacy means to you in your life and work. In that last paper you should discuss explicitly how your personal attitudes affect, shape, or complicate your approach to teaching writing. (David, "Practicum Syllabus")

The two drafts of the literacy narratives the graduate instructors at Public wrote provided a forum for them to consider and reflect on the understandings of literacy they brought to the course, a reflection I argue is crucial to their development as teachers. For the most part, the revisions to the final narratives brought with them a critical perspective and a self-reflexivity that, although not completely developed, demonstrate the beginning of a learning trajectory whereby the graduate instructors were interrogating past views and experiences in light of new understandings. As I discuss at the end of chapter 3, for example, the graduate instructors who viewed textual appreciation and analysis as their main teaching goal began to negotiate how they could still value texts while resisting the hierarchies implicit in cultural-literacy conception. I agree with Restaino's (2012) contention that opportunities for reflection might not easily arise during graduate instructors' chaotic first semester; the graduate instructors represented here did not have sufficient time to think through the implications of their positions. However, they were beginning this process. These narratives took a step toward allowing them to, as Welch (1993) says, "identify and question their own taken-for-granted assumptions . . . *as assumptions*, as historically situated and politically informed ways of constructing and understanding teaching and learning" (398–99). In other words, one of the goals of the practicum should be to provide space for reflection while at the same time making the familiar strange and disrupting graduate instructors' tendency to codify. The benefits of literacy-narrative assignments are supported by research on graduate-teacher education. Suresh Canagarajah (2016) argues that because of its possibilities in "contribut[ing] to teacher identity development," the literacy narrative should play a central role in the graduate practicum (268). As in the practicum at Public, Canagarajah (2016) asks graduate instructors to revise their narratives in response to comments he has given them throughout the semester and include this final draft in a portfolio submitted at the end (269). This document, and its revision, facilitates graduate instructors' renegotiation of attitudes and practices they had previously taken for granted.

Of course, literacy narratives can have drawbacks as well. Alexander (2011) contends that student literacy narratives tend to draw unknowingly on "dominant, archetypal narratives," (609), many of which affirm rather than challenge what Harvey Graff and John Duffy (2008) call "literacy myths," such as the idea of literacy as the means to economic or cultural success (41). An example of such a myth would be the "great-divide" theory of literacy that shows up in the narratives written by the graduate students in literary studies (see chapter 3), in which individuals familiar with the canon or other elevated works are perceived as literate, while undergraduates unfamiliar with these texts are not.

Grutsch McKinney and Chiseri-Strater (2003) also warn that narratives do "not always provide the whole story" of how new teachers' identities are developing, cautioning that graduate instructors may be performing the selves they believe they *should be* (60). Yet, I argue there is value in getting graduate instructors to articulate these myths and idealized selves. At many points in their narratives, even as they were writing stories that were conforming to preexisting literacy tropes and narratives, graduate instructors began to sense that something was fishy about their own stories. One of the most obvious examples is in Garrett's first literacy narrative, in which he begins to interrogate his hierarchical views of literacy in the context of his relationships with his grandmother and his friend Quinn. Garrett states,

> Though I try not to judge my grandmother for reading detective fiction, I do. Of course, she sits on some imaginary level above people who do not care to read at all, but this imaginary level is still an ethical failure on her part. The irony, of course, is that my grandmother taught me to like reading and Quinn taught me to fear it. ("Literacy Narrative Draft," 2010)

Although one could certainly take the fact of Garrett's judging his grandmother, a woman who has given him so much, literally, as I argue in chapter 3, I don't think he invokes this story to portray such a clear-cut view. Rather, Garrett's reference to "irony" suggests he is beginning the process of questioning why he would hold a view of literacy that so clearly marginalizes his grandmother as a literate individual. His admission ("I do") is, I believe, part of a process toward articulating a more forgiving view of literacy, one in which he, his grandmother, Quinn, and now his composition students can all occupy the same literacy plane. As he stated in his initial interview with me, "We're all climbing the same hill here" (pers. comm., October 20, 2010).

A crucial part of the graduate instructors' reflection upon their past experiences happened when they met with me for their interviews and with David to think about possible ways for developing their literacy narratives. Indeed, my interviews with the graduate instructors prompted them to articulate their literacy and teaching philosophies and begin the process of questioning prior views. As Estrem and Reid (2012) found in their study, the graduate instructors were "using the interview as a processing space" (464). Without these interventions, Jordi might not have realized the profound influence her father had on her literacy development. Max might not have seen the connection between his poetry's subversion of academic citation conventions and his attitudes towards teaching his students these same conventions. Barbara began to appreciate, during our interview, the social and gendered nature of her literacy conception and to see how it worked together with ideas articulated in the readings of the practicum course. As I note in chapter 2, one of the most dramatic results from one of the interviews came in Karen's revised literacy narrative, in which she reconsiders both her previous interpretation of the Jarratt article she had read in the practicum and the parallels between her struggles and her students'. Without my prompting to look again at Jarratt's article and to reexamine whether, like Karen, her students might also feel they would like more choice in what they were writing about, Karen might not have come to a crucial realization about herself as a teacher.

Although I argue throughout this book for the power of the conceptions of literacy and the comparatively small (and brief) role of the practicum, the opportunities for reflection I describe have the potential to have much longer-term effects on graduate instructors. When I was about to end the conversation with Lily that begins this chapter, she said something that surprised me:

> I tell David, I always think of Meaghan's perception of me as personal and spiritual and how I've changed. It's one of the points in my opening talk [for my dissertation defense] . . . I never would have seen it otherwise, if I hadn't signed up for the study. I would have just kept going along, not questioning it. I guess part of it is I'm trying to think about that in terms of my own work now. For the average person, a conception of literacy is so compartmentalized—for me, as an English teacher, it affects everything (pers. comm., September 26, 2010)

While I give Lily more credit than she gives herself here (I don't think she would have "just kept going along, not questioning it"), her statement points to the importance of giving graduate instructors carefully structured opportunities to examine their preexisting views. In this case, again, her participation in a study in which I was interpreting her views also raised a mirror to her conception of literacy. That is, reading about herself from another person's perspective made possible a realization that might otherwise have taken more time or happened in a different way.

I should note here that such mirror raising must be done with care. Welch's (1993) account of her experience as a newish graduate instructor demonstrates how damaging having someone label your worldview can be, especially if it is done smugly or is accompanied by a repeated questioning of your beliefs. Welch describes, for example, overhearing herself being labeled as a "freewriter" and also having an instructor respond suggestively to her statement about whose theories of writing she relied on: "Oh, so *you* like Peter Elbow" (390–91). Thus, while WPAs, practica instructors, and mentors should directly help new graduate instructors interpret their views of literacy, we should take care not to appear glib or superior.

One way mentors and others can convey their sincere desire to help new graduate instructors is by admitting to not knowing everything about writing, literacy, or pedagogy—acknowledging, as I imagine many of us do in our other classes, areas where we might be weak or problems we still occasionally encounter in our teaching. This is not to say we must undermine the fact of our having knowledge and experience. Composition experts know things about teaching composition, and we can introduce some of these things to new graduate instructors in the practicum. However, we can also identify with graduate instructors if we have experienced some of the same problems. For example, Barbara's discussion with me about race (not knowing how to get especially her international students and students of color to talk) prompted me to respond that I still have trouble initiating productive conversations about race in the classroom. Allowing graduate instructors to see areas we are still exploring and that we are still attempting to improve our teaching might also open up opportunities to investigate new approaches together.

Although the curriculum for the practicum at Public facilitated some productive discussions about literacy, it could have done more to support graduate instructors' grappling with how their conceptions were influencing their teaching. For one, almost none of the readings for the course directly discussed theories of literacy. Graduate instructors did read texts that discussed more than writing (like David Jolliffe and Allison Harl's article [2008] on reading and numerous articles on race). However, I would have added, early in the course, readings I have since used successfully with undergraduates, including two I used in developing the theoretical frame for the study informing this book. Scribner's (1984) "Literacy in Three Metaphors" describes and notes boundary issues with viewing literacy as adaptation, power, and a state of grace. Knoblauch's "Literacy and the Politics of Education" (1990) points similarly to definitional difficulties surrounding literacy and describes what he terms "functionalist literacy," "cultural literacy," "literacy for personal growth," and "critical literacy." Both readings are accessible (I've taught them to undergraduates from first-year to upper-level courses) and create a vocabulary for students as we discuss literacy views throughout the semester. (For example, a student, responding to another student during a recent class discussion said, "Well, I guess this is very cultural literacy of me, but . . .") Given the typical semester-long time frame of the practicum course and the many issues that must be addressed within this short time frame, I would only use one of these readings, perhaps pairing it with something like Gee's (1989) "Literacy, Discourse, and Linguistics" (as a way of getting graduate instructors to identify the discourses they belong to) or Brandt's (1998) "Sponsors of Literacy."

A second issue is that because the graduate instructors turned in their revised literacy narrative at the end of the semester, they did not get the chance to compare and analyze the two versions of their literacy narratives. If the graduate instructors could have examined their revised literacy narrative with the distance of a few weeks, they might have seen more than they did by just producing it and their final teaching portfolio, which probably took place in a flurry of other seminar papers they had to write. A follow-up activity to the submission of these revised narratives might be to return them and ask the graduate instructors to reflect on the literacy values they see at work in them. In hindsight, it might have been useful if I had returned the portfolios and given them the opportunity to sit down with the coding guide I developed for conceptions of literacy and see where they might place themselves and why.

Another strategy to get new graduate instructors to engage more fully both with the field of composition and their own knowing and not knowing is to encourage them to create and revise their teaching materials and the materials of the graduate practicum. Of course, new graduate instructors generally want to have access to already-developed teaching materials; to have to develop their own syllabus and assignments would be too much for graduate instructors during a first semester in which they are just trying to stay afloat. That is, new graduate instructors appreciate "practical" instruction, including lesson plans and activities that can be easily picked up or modified for their own use (see Guerra and Bawarshi 2005; Rupiper Taggart and Lowry 2011, 95). At the same time, they also want the freedom and ability to insert themselves into their courses, modifying materials so they make sense in terms of the graduate teachers' own frameworks and developing materials collaboratively with their peers, as Barbara and Karen from the current study frequently did (Grouling 2015; Rupiper Taggart and Lowry 2011). Thus, one way to honor the knowledge new graduate instructors bring to the table would be for practica to assign each graduate instructor to collaboratively develop and present activities they used in their classroom. This activity would give presenters the opportunity to improve activities and recognize the assumptions about literacy informing them. For example, as I discuss in chapter 3, asking graduate instructors in literary studies to present lessons geared toward close reading can be an opportunity to push them to also think of ways to situate close reading as just one reading strategy among many.

A final concern related to graduate instructors' formal pedagogy education is the curricula of the courses the graduate instructors are teaching. Although the syllabus for CC at Public created opportunities for the graduate instructors to bring their interests and expertise into the class—which is crucial as new graduate instructors develop a sense of autonomy and authority in the classroom—it didn't provide much space for graduate instructors to find out about *their* students attitudes' towards literacy beyond the surface-level sense they got of their students' resistance to reading, writing, and revising. At many points in this study, I noted moments of effacement, which Dryer (2012) describes as moments when graduate students deny that undergraduates in the same situation as they are could have similar motives, experiences, or feelings (438–39). Effacement was evident in Karen's denial that her students could be feeling ambivalence toward academic writing or that they might, like her, appreciate more opportunity for choice in their assignments. However, if these graduate instructors were talking about literacy alongside their students, they might be less apt to flatten their students' experiences.

For example, since observing the graduate instructors at Public grappling with but not entirely understanding Bartholomae's (1985) "Inventing the University," I have taught this essay to undergraduates in composition courses at other universities. I am always struck by the insights into their experiences these undergraduates emerge with. Even when I'm teaching advanced and honors sections of composition, the undergraduates give the impression of being more willing than the graduate instructors to assume a novice stance and admit to having some of the same struggles as the students in Bartholomae's article. If the graduate instructors had been given the opportunity to both teach this text in their classes *and* discuss it in the practicum, they might have emerged with a deeper understanding not only of key concepts that have become foundational in composition studies (such as the understanding of writing as social, situated, and discourse specific) but also of how their experiences have paralleled their students'. In other words, hearing what their students had to say about articles such as these might have allowed them to see the concepts, the experiences of their students, and their own experiences in more textured, complex ways. Moreover, by engaging their students in discussions about literacy and allowing opportunities for both themselves and their students to bring in their experiences with literacy as evidence to inform their interpretations, they might have been impressed with the insights their students yielded.

FINAL THOUGHTS: OUR LITERACY
CONCEPTIONS, OURSELVES

As I discuss in the previous chapter, making literacy more central both to both the graduate practicum and the composition courses graduate instructors teach might also involve shifting our priorities and even our sense of disciplinary identity. We have arrived, I think, at a critical juncture in our field where the need to articulate what we know feels urgent and necessary. I am particularly convinced by chapters by Hansen (2018) and Maher (2018) in Malenczyk et al.'s *Rhetoric, Composition, and Disciplinarity*, in which they argue that our discipline has generated a large body of knowledge over the past fifty years and that we should not acquiesce to the "continued institutional denial of [compositionists'] disciplinary expertise" (Maher 2018, 173).

At the same time, we must think more deeply about what, as a field, we still need to know and how much of what we know must be articulated to novices. As Smit (2004) argues, we must return to questions that are fundamental to how we define ourselves as a field but that we have yet to satisfactorily answer, questions like, What is writing and writing ability? What does it mean to be a teacher of writing? And while answering these questions is likely to involve new research, we don't necessarily need to reinvent some of the knowledge that will help us answer them. Indeed, if we look to fields like linguistics and literacy studies, some of the answers, or at least some better ways of framing these questions, already exist.

In *The Lure of Literacy*, Michael Harker (2015) argues that returning to the insights of new literacy studies has the potential to make assumptions about the first-year course (and, I would add, the education of new graduate instructors) that are often unacknowledged explicit. Too often, teachers and researchers assume literacy is "well-traveled ground" in scholarship in composition and engage with it only superficially (4–5). Yet examining the experiences of new graduate instructors through the lens of literacy theory reveals the very real, human dimensions of what it means to teach writing and, particularly, what it means to be a new teacher. Conceptions of literacy not only undergird our first-year courses and writing programs but are a determining factor in the day-to-day decisions we make about what to teach. Having a concept for literacy, understanding it as ideology, and bringing a conceptions-of-literacy lens to understanding ourselves as teachers helps us see our personal investments in literacy, providing a way forward to creating more effective and reflective courses.

Perhaps channeling tensions about our discipline, Reid (2007) states of her own position as a WPA, "And that leaves me anxious about my own position as an ambassador of the field's best new ideas to the uninitiated graduate students who enter my classes and concerned about whether 'the field' can or should agree on how much of its expertise needs to be interpolated into introductory pedagogies" (248). While it would be hubris to suggest we can easily resolve these tensions (and quell our anxieties about graduate-instructor education), I hope the conceptions-of-literacy framework offers some suggestions for how practica instructors and WPAs can work productively within them.

APPENDIX A
Descriptions of Instruments and Data Analysis

1. Literacy Narratives

Participants wrote two drafts of a literacy narrative in response to a required assignment for the practicum. David had used the literacy narrative in the past as a tool to elicit reflection in the practicum course, so he offered to build this particular component into the course. The assignment, which he wrote, was as follows:

> Following the theme of conceptions of literacy, I'll ask you to write a brief literacy narrative for the September 10 class and a longer literacy reflection paper due on the last day of class. In the shorter narrative (3–5 pages), please detail an experience, an interaction with another person, or a memory that is emblematic for you of your attitude toward reading and writing. This first paper will serve as a starting point for your contemplation of literacy as a force or a phenomenon in your life. I will not grade this paper but I will respond to it extensively, noting possible themes to explore. I'd like you to return to the topic in your longer reflection paper (7–10 pages), and be sure to consider BOTH reading and writing as you come to a more articulated understanding of what literacy means to you in your life and work. In that last paper you should discuss explicitly how your personal attitudes affect, shape, or complicate your approach to teaching writing. ("Practicum Syllabus")

These two narratives (the initial literacy narrative and the revised, final narrative) gave me a glimpse not only into the experiences with and ideas about literacy the graduate instructors brought with them to the practicum course and their first semester of teaching but also into how, if at all, they changed throughout the semester.

DOI: 10.7330/9781607329343.c006

2. Interviews

I also asked participants specific questions about their literacy experiences during three open-ended, semistructured interviews (see appendix B). I employed the technique of stimulated recall by asking participants to send me, in advance of our first interview, two pieces of writing, one they wrote for school and one written outside school. Although I recognize these instructions might have limited the possibilities for what the graduate instructors brought in by depicting literacy largely in terms of writing, I felt the need to set some constraints on what they brought in for a few reasons. First, I reasoned that, because they were graduate students, writing had played an influential role in their literacy development and that, as with the instructors Dryer (2012) discusses, for many of them it would be the source of powerful feelings. Second, because writing, and by extension literacy, is inherently multimodal, I also saw these graduate instructors' writing as ways to get at other, non-text-based aspects of their literacy experiences.

3. Assignment-Ranking Activity

I also checked participants' conceptions using a ranking activity I constructed and then administered during one of the practicum meetings (see appendix C). For the activity, I wrote six assignments, with each assignment matching one of the conceptions I was examining and coding for. In the practicum, I asked the graduate instructors to rank the assignments from 1 to 6, with one meaning they would most likely to assign this kind of paper and 6 least likely. I also asked them to briefly discuss their rationale for their rankings and told them they could also make notes in the margins to explain their decisions. Once they were finished, we discussed the assignments as a class. This discussion gave me a good reading on how the class was interpreting the assignments and whether the assignments were good measures of the literacy conceptions.

4. Classroom Observations

I observed each of the seven focal participants twice, once in the fall of 2010 and then again in the spring of 2011. After each classroom observation, I presented participants with handwritten field notes I had taken as I observed them teaching their College Composition class. Together, we examined the notes as I shared with the participants what I had observed, asking them to identify decisions they had made in their teaching and discuss them with me.

5. Field Notes of Practicum Meetings

Finally, I attended all the practicum class meetings with the exception of one to take notes on participants' comments and participation in class and to be able to describe the context of the practicum. In order to make my appearance less intrusive, I did not tape record these sessions, but I did take detailed field notes, making sure to get down as much of what was said as possible and then typing up and taking notes on what I had witnessed immediately following each practicum session.

DATA ANALYSIS

In order to investigate the content of the data I gathered, following Michael Smith and Dorothy Strickland, I parsed the data into content units, which they define as "segments of discourse designed to make a single point" (Smith and Strickland 2001, 150). I coded the units in qualitative management system software Altas.ti, using the seven categories I discuss in chapter 1: literacy for personal growth, literacy for social growth, social/critical literacy, critical-activist literacy, cultural literacy, functionalist literacy, and instrumental literacy. As the table in appendix D indicates, each of these categories acted as larger classifications for what was actually a constellation of beliefs about literacy that informed each participant's conception. For example, a code for cultural literacy could correspond to a moment in the data when a participant referred to a particularly text-based notion of literacy, to a reference to the importance of studying classic texts, or to a sense of literacy as marking someone's insider status.

At a few points, I had to make decisions about how to code content units that could have been indicative of more than one literacy perspective. When considering how to code these borderline cases, it was most helpful for me to view the six categories as each attending to a particular *dimension* of literacy. In Burke's (1966) discussion of terministic screens, he argues that, as ideological visions of the world, each individual's screen "directs the attention to one field [of language] rather than another" (50). For example, literacy for social growth and cultural literacy are similar in that both see literacy as the vehicle for a shared cultural vision. However, whereas literacy for social growth privileges the *social* dimension of literacy, cultural literacy privileges the *text*. Similarly, although both cultural literacy and literacy for personal growth see literacy as the means for transcendence, for cultural literacy, understanding the *text* is the end result, whereas in literacy for personal growth, it is an understanding of one's *self*.

Once I coded the data, I used the query tool in Atlas.ti to look for patterns and co-occurrences. During these queries, I gained new insights about the data and the conceptions. For example, I initially did not know how to connect the frequent references of the three graduate instructors in literature to "texts" and "close reading." However, once I noticed these references occurred contiguously with data coded *cultural literacy*, I began to see the elevation of texts as part of cultural literacy.

APPENDIX B
Interview Protocol

Demographic Questions

1. What is your current age?
2. What race or ethnicity do you identify as?
3. What did your parent(s) and/or guardian(s) do for a living?
4. Where did you attend high school?
5. What kind of high school (public, Catholic, etc.) did you attend?
6. Where did you go to college?
7. When did you decide that you wanted to go to graduate school? What prompted this decision?

Stimulated Recall Interview

1. Tell me a bit about this piece of writing.
2. What prompted this piece of writing?
3. In the first piece, you talk about _____. Can you tell me more about that?
4. You also discuss_____. What do you mean by ____ here?
5. What kind of audience did you imagine for this piece?
6. What might this piece tell your reader about who you are?
7. What are you doing in this piece of writing that you would want students in your class to do in their writing?
8. What would you not want students in your class to do?
9. Let's switch gears now and look at your second piece of writing. How would you compare this piece of writing to the first?
10. Tell me a bit about the process of writing the second piece.

DOI: 10.7330/9781607329343.c007

11. Both the first and the second piece of writing _____. Can you talk about the significance of _____ in your writing?

12. What kind of audience did you imagine for this second piece?

13. What might this piece tell your reader about who you are?

14. What are you doing in this piece of writing that you would want students in your class to do in their writing?

15. What would you *not* want students in your class to do?

APPENDIX C
Assignment-Ranking Activity

Below I have included six writing assignments. Rank these according to which you think you would most want to assign in your class (1) to least want to assign (6). You may want to make notes in the margins to explain your ranking. Once you're done ranking, write down a brief rationale for why you ranked the assignments as you did.

_____ *Assignment 1*

The concept of Manifest Destiny is a defining part of American culture—knowledge of which all literate Americans should have. For Leslie Marmon Silko, for example, understanding this idea is essential because it impacts the way we think about our national borders. Your task for this assignment is to demonstrate that understanding Manifest Destiny is essential to Americans' cultural identity in the twenty-first century by identifying one way this idea has shaped our culture today. You should consider a current issue in which an understanding of Manifest Destiny might aid the public's understanding of that issue. Your thesis should answer the question, Why should every American know about Manifest Destiny?

[cultural literacy]

_____ *Assignment 2*

Our readings on the frontier movement in American history have prompted us to consider the following questions: What does it mean to be American? In what ways do the qualities of Americanism described by authors like Turner still typify Americans today? What happens when we view these characteristics of Americanism from a different cultural perspective from our own?

DOI: 10.7330/9781607329343.c008

The goal of this assignment is to expand these problems beyond the walls of the classroom and consider them in the context of the many cultural communities . . . [surrounding Public U.] You will sign up to volunteer for Project Shine, a program in which volunteers tutor older adult immigrants who are studying to pass the citizenship exam. . . . After you have spent ten hours volunteering over the course of the next several weeks, you will write a reflective essay in which you discuss how your experiences challenged your ideas about Americanism and culture.

[critical-activism literacy]

_____ **Assignment 3**

Both Leslie Marmon Silko and Jane Tompkins write about disturbing experiences that nevertheless end up producing some sort of revelation or new insight. Choose one of these essays and reread it, paying close attention to Silko and/or Tompkins's personal reactions to what they were seeing and hearing. Then, write an essay in which you compare either experience to a similar experience you had. How were your reactions similar to and/or different from Silko's or Tompkins's? What do you think accounts for these differences or similarities?

[literacy for personal growth]

_____ **Assignment 4**

For this assignment, you will be asked to practice the writing skills we have gone over in class. The assignment should summarize the key points of Patricia Nelson Limerick's essay, "Denial and Dependence." To do this, you should carefully go over the passage, identifying Limerick's main points. Then, you should *summarize these points in your own words.* Follow this summary with a *close reading* of one or two paragraphs of the essay that illustrate these points. Because this is a close reading, you should pay careful attention to the words Limerick uses and how they contribute to her tone and voice. In the close reading section, make sure that you use quotes, documented according to MLA format, and quote/paraphrase combinations. Remember to carefully check your paper for grammar and correctness before handing it in.

[functionalist literacy]

_____ **Assignment 5**

Our readings on the frontier movement in American history have prompted us to consider the following questions: What does it mean to be American? In what ways do the qualities of Americanism described by authors like Turner still typify Americans today? What happens when we view these characteristics of Americanism from a different cultural perspective from our own?

For this assignment, you should identify the key words and ideas Turner associates with Americanism. What traits needed for frontier survival contributed to these ideas? After considering this, in a few paragraphs, choose one of these ideas and think about one of two specific ways this idea is present in our culture today. How does acceptance of this idea mark someone as being American? You may wish to consider a personal experience to illustrate this.

[literacy for social growth]

_____ **Assignment 6**

In "The American West and the Burden of Belief," N. Scott Momaday writes that "Our human tendency is to concentrate the word on a stage" (627). And though this view of the world, and in this case the West, "fascinates us" it is also "a distorted view of the West" (627). For this assignment, you should write a critical essay in which you analyze Momaday's views on the mythologization of the West and the "narcissism of the European tradition" (627). Then, respond to Momaday's argument by viewing a film featuring elements of the West. You should use specific instances from the film to support your analysis.

[critical literacy]

APPENDIX D
Coding Protocol

Conception of literacy/ coding family	Characteristics of conception/ individual codes	Representative examples from the data, excerpted from content units
Personal growth	- emphasis on self, self-determination - voice - authenticity - power of the individual imagination - expressive writing - personalized reading programs - whole-language curricula - teacher as nurturer	"Learning to write was realizing that I could all along" (Lily, "Literacy Narrative Final," 2010).
Social growth	- personal growth/attainment as a means for social progress, social awareness, social understanding - understanding role in society - literacy as empathy - aspects of social/critical but deemphasizes or moderates fight for social change, focusing instead on changing individuals first	"So, I want them to be able to empathize with what it was like to be, you know, an Indian under British rule or just to be alive in the world then and see that it's really not that different" (Barbara, pers. comm., October 26, 2010).
Social/ critical	- realization of potential to create change - writing in order to resist - awareness of language as socially situated - understanding of language/ speakers as always being "interested" - language as ideology - literacy as power - Marxist philosophical premises	"I began to change my perception of reading from a solitary activity to a communal one that, while still done alone, could be an invitation to conversations about books and ideas" (Barbara, "Literacy Narrative Final," 2010).

continued on next page

DOI: 10.7330/9781607329343.c009

continued

Conception of literacy/ coding family	Characteristics of conception/ individual codes	Representative examples from the data, excerpted from content units
Social/ activist	- creation of opportunities for meaningful contribution to a community - literacy to bring about radical political reform	"I think being able to work with people in [the area around Public] will make everything more meaningful, visceral, and applicable. I don't know if I am biased because I worked with these populations, but I find it gives you a sense of understanding/inspiration/heart experience" (Lily, Assignment-Ranking Activity, October 22, 2010).
Functionalist literacy	- tying of literacy to concrete needs (careers) - language as a value-neutral medium - basic-skills literacy - efficiency - current-traditional rhetoric - socioeconomic benefits of literacy - acquisition of skills - material production - need for writing skills in the modern information economy - emphasis on grammar	"I do circle their editing errors, but I say that I don't want to emphasize those things, but I do want to call attention to them. The missing hyphen in African American just drove me crazy!" (Karen, pers. comm., October 26, 2010)

Instrumental literacy	- study of language/form to demystify academic writing
	- learning of rules of various discourse communities
	- teaching of genre knowledge/ transfer of writing skills
	- ability to refer to the following from functionalist literacy, but with a critical or reflective emphasis:
	  o tying of literacy to con-crete needs (careers)
	  o need for writing skills in the modern information economy
		"That's to me what the job of first-year writing is, in my mind. Preparing them to be successful in college. You know, writing for a college audience" (Karen, pers. comm., November 19, 2010).

continued on next page

continued

Conception of literacy/ coding family	Characteristics of conception/ individual codes	Representative examples from the data, excerpted from content units
Cultural literacy	- "Great Books" or the canon - capacity for higher-order thinking - fears of a fall from grace or decline of literacy - marginalization of noncanonical or popular works - close reading - emphasis on text, text-based understanding of literacy - view of students' texts as deficient - taste and aesthetic appreciation of texts - religious or ritualistic understanding of literacy	"Because a discussion has to start somewhere? Because ideas are important? I don't know. I mean, that's a really hard question, and it's definitely something I take for granted. Like the text is the thing. That's where you start" (Jordi, pers. comm., March 14, 2010).

APPENDIX E
Practicum Schedule of Topics and Readings

Course Texts

Barnett, Timothy, ed. 2002. *Teaching Argument in the Composition Course.* Boston: Bedford/St. Martin's.

Glenn, Cheryl and Melissa A. Goldthwaite, eds. 2008. *The St. Martin's Guide to Teaching Writing,* 6th ed. Boston: Bedford/St. Martin's.

Week	Topics	Readings
1	MACRO: What is a teacher? Intro to FYW MICRO: Reading mark-ups, responding to student papers, research project	Glenn, chapter 2, "The First Few Days of Class" Student portfolios
2	MACRO: Conceptions of literacy MICRO: Lesson planning, groups, leading discussion, summary	Glenn, chapter 3, "Everyday Activities" David A. Jolliffe and Allison Harl, "Texts of Our Institutional Lives"
3	MACRO: Theories of Reading MICRO: Interpreting primary documents, peer review, teaching citation	David Bartholomae, "Inventing the University" Mariolina Salvatori, "The 'Argument of Reading' in the Teaching of Composition" (Barnett 346)
4	MACRO: Responding to student writing and cognitive/emotional development MICRO: Writing comments, conferencing, "correcting"	Glenn, chapter 5, "Evaluating Student Essays" Wendy Bishop, "Helping Peer Writing Groups Succeed" (Glenn 343) Nancy Sommers, "Responding to Student Writing" (Glenn 352)
5	MACRO: Argumentation MICRO: Conferencing for revision	Andrea A. Lunsford and Cheryl Glenn, "Rhetorical Theory and the Teaching of Writing" (Glenn 452) Chaim Perelman and Lucie Olbrechts-Tyteca, "From the New Rhetoric" (Barnett 132)

continued on next page

DOI: 10.7330/9781607329343.c010

continued

Week	Topics	Readings
6	Macro: Research Micro: Preparing for Assignment 3, grammar workshop	Glenn, chapter 9, "Teaching Memory" Patrick Hartwell, "Grammar, Grammars, and the Teaching of Grammar" (Glenn 305)
7	Macro: Invention and revision Micro: Mid-term assessments	Glenn, chapter 6, "Teaching Invention"
8	Macro: Multiculturalism and race Micro: Responding to Assignment 2	Jacqueline Royster, "When the First Voice You Hear is Not Your Own" (Glenn 371) Beverly J. Moss and Keith Walters, "Rethinking Diversity" (Glenn 417) Peggy McIntosh, "White Privilege: Unpacking the Invisible Napsack"
9	Macro: Assignment design and teaching the book length text Micro: Connections between *Cultural Conversations* and *Kindred*	Glenn, chapter 4, "Successful Writing Assignments" Patrick J. Slattery, "The Argumentative, Multiple-Source Paper" (Barnett 361)
10	Macro: Holistic grading and learning differences Micro: Steering students as they choose topics	Lynn Z. Bloom, "Why I Used to Hate to Give Grades" (Glenn 361) Jay Dolmage, "Mapping Composition: Inviting Disability in the Front Door" Amy Vidali, "Discourse of Disability and Basic Writing"
11	Macro: Managing controversy and embracing diversity Micro: Hot button issues in *Kindred*	Bruce Horner and John Trimbur, "English Only and U.S. College Composition" (Glenn 505) Kevin Michael Deluca, "Unruly Arguments" (Barnett 225)
12	Mock Portfolio Review	
13	Macro: Assessment and reflection Micro: Conclusion of the semester, syllabus construction	Susan Jarratt, "Feminism and Composition: The Case for Conflict."

NOTES

CHAPTER 1. INTRODUCTION

1. Tina Lavonne Good and Leanne Warshauer (2000) also found, through a survey of journal articles in composition, that most composition courses are staffed by graduate instructors, adjuncts, or graduate instructors as adjuncts (x).

2. Although most studies refer to graduate students who are acting as instructors of record for composition courses as *graduate teaching assistants* (*GTAs*), this study refers to them as *graduate instructors* to recognize they are not "assisting" some other instructor but are rather fully responsible for managing their own courses (see Schell 1998, 165).

3. My review of the research suggests that Public U's model of graduate-instructor mentoring and education is typical; studies by Bishop (1990), Rankin (1994), Dryer (2012), and Obermark, Brewer, and Halasek (2015) all report similar models. Indeed, Stephen Wilhoit (2002) argues that the "pre-service orientation" plus "in-service coursework or practica in composition pedagogy or theory" are the two most common features of graduate-instructor education (17–18). Other programs, such as the one at George Mason mentioned by Reid, Estrem, and Belcheir (2012), require a year of tutoring in a university writing center prior to the first semester of teaching. At Public, some graduate students in this study had a year or two of working as teaching assistants for large survey courses in literature taught by full-time faculty before teaching their own classes. Graduate students who entered their programs with master's degrees and had prior college-level teaching experience were not required to take the practicum.

4. This ended up being impossible because the only two comp/rhet students in the class were women. Because of this imbalance, I asked Blake, who identified as male, to participate in an attempt to balance the gender distribution.

5. Of the eighteen graduate instructors enrolled in the practicum, all identified as Caucasian, with the exception of one graduate instructor who identified as Asian American and another who identified as half Asian.

6. In Goggin's (2008) study, he applies his categories to a sampling of articles from 1994 to 2004 on computers and composition from six major journals (xv).

7. Scribner's (1984) literacy categories, which she calls "metaphors," are the oldest and include three ways of seeing literacy: literacy as adaptation, literacy as power, and literacy as a state of grace. Knoblauch (1990) renames and adds to Scribner's metaphors, terming literacy as adaptation "functionalist literacy" and literacy as power "critical literacy." Literacy as a state of grace gets split into two categories: literacy for personal growth and cultural literacy. Goggin (2008), finally, adds three more categories

to Knoblauch's: functional literacy, critical-activism literacy, and literacy for social growth.

8. Although I argue that social/critical literacy is the dominant ideological construct informing composition's thinking about pedagogy, critical pedagogy has been challenged. Richard Miller (1998), for example, questions why composition instructors "continue to deploy [Freire's rhetoric] long after our own experiences have demonstrated its inutility" (12). Feminist theorists have pointed out that Freire has become yet another male "hero" teacher figure (Gramer 2017, 122).

9. This attitude is unfortunate given that Kendall Leon, Laurie Pinker, and Kathryn Trauth Taylor (2017) describe how beneficial community-based or service-learning pedagogies (which I categorize within the critical-activist framework) can be not only for composition students but also for instructor learning (Leon, Pinker, and Taylor 2017).

10. These home-based identities are influenced by sponsors and discourse communities outside the home. See Gee's (1989) concept of "filtering" for more information (15).

CHAPTER 2. YOGA ASHRAMS AND MOTHER-TEACHERS

1. See, for example, *Critical Expressivism: Theory and Practice in the Composition Classroom*, edited by Tara Roeder and Roseanne Gatto and Chris Burnham and Rebecca Powell's chapter in *A Guide to Composition Pedagogies* (Roeder and Gatto 2015; Burnham and Powell 2013).

2. As with any attempt to quantify qualitative data, these numbers alone do not represent the whole story. They are skewed by the fact that I assigned more codes to Lily's data than to any other participant's: her data had a total of 215 codes, with Jordi coming in next at 171 codes. Because 67.4 percent of the codes in Lily's data were for literacy for personal growth, the largest percentage any of the participants had for any one code, this category might seem more ubiquitous than it was.

3. See, for example, statements made by David Coleman (2011), the president of the College Board.

4. Elbow (1998) describes the believing game as a way to counter the main way he argues academics find truth, which is by "seeking error" or doubting (148). By contrast, to play the believing game is to "Believe all assertions," which allows the teacher (or peer reviewer) to understand and identify with the writer (148).

CHAPTER 3. TEXTS, HIERARCHY, AND RITUAL

1. For example, Cole and Lyon (2008) argue that graduate instructors who buy into this way of seeing literacy tend to "spend days discussing literature and never mention student texts" (196). Bishop (1995) argues similarly, saying many graduate students are "life-long readers who have

consumed text after text" and, consequently, maybe feel uncomfortable teaching a course that focuses on textual production rather than consumption (440).

2. I have written more extensively about the hierarchical relationship between composition and literary studies elsewhere (see Brewer and di Gennaro 2018).

3. The early (initial draft of the) narratives had 73 content units I coded for one of the seven conceptions, whereas the later, revised narratives had 168.

CHAPTER 4. GRADUATE INSTRUCTORS AT THE THRESHOLD

1. As Aubrey Schiavone and Anna V. Knutson discuss, Max's choice to attend a university because of its proximity rather than its reputation is another marker of someone coming from a working-class background (Schiavone and Knutson 2017, 32).

CHAPTER 5. CONCLUSION

1. The one response I coded *other* was when Jordi referred to finding an idea for a lesson online when she typed in "different ways to start an intro" (pers. comm., October 20, 2010).

   As Estrem and Reid (2012) say of the numerical data in their study, I don't think these numbers support fine-grained analysis. However, when contextualized with the other data, as well as with other studies of graduate instructors' experiences as new teachers, they do point to the influence of graduate instructors' prior conceptions on their teaching.

2. I should note that whereas I chose to make this a separate category from the practicum, I could also make a case for combining this category with the practicum, given that the standard syllabus was the one officially sanctioned by the practicum and the FYWP.

REFERENCES

Adler-Kassner, Linda. 2012. "The Companies We Keep or the Companies We Would Like to Try to Keep: Strategies and Tactics in Challenging Times." *WPA: Writing Program Administration* 36 (1): 119–40.

Adler-Kassner, Linda. 2018. "Looking Outward: Disciplinarity and Dialogue in Landscapes of Practice." In *Composition, Rhetoric, and Disciplinarity*, edited by Rita Malenczyk, Susan Miller-Cochran, Elizabeth Wardle, and Kathleen Blake Yancey, 303–30. Logan: Utah State University Press.

Adler-Kassner, Linda, John Majewski, and Damian Koshnick. 2012. "The Value of Troublesome Knowledge." *Composition Forum* 26. http://compositionforum.com/issue/26/troublesome-knowledge-threshold.php.

Adler-Kassner, Linda, and Elizabeth Wardle. 2015. *Naming What We Know: Threshold Concepts of Writing Studies*. Logan: Utah State University Press.

Adler-Kassner, Linda, and Elizabeth Wardle. 2016. "What Are Threshold Concepts (and Why Are They Useful for Writing Programs)?" In *A Rhetoric for Writing Program Administrators*, 2nd ed., edited by Rita Malenczyk, 64–77. Anderson, SC: Parlor Press.

Alexander, Jonathan, Eli Goldblatt, Angela M. Haas, Paula Mathieu, and Jacqueline Rhodes. 2017. "Naming What WE Know: A Roundtable on Knowledge Production in Composition." Conference on College Composition and Communication, Portland, OR, March 17.

Alexander, Kara Poe. 2011. "Successes, Victims, and Prodigies: 'Master' and 'Little' Cultural Narratives in the Literacy Narrative Genre." *College Composition and Communication* 62 (4): 608–33.

Anson, Chris. 2015. "Crossing Thresholds: What's to Know about Writing across the Curriculum." In *Naming What We Know: Threshold Concepts of Writing Studies*, edited by Linda Adler-Kassner and Elizabeth Wardle, 203–19. Logan: Utah State University Press.

Ball, Cheryl E., and Colin Charlton. 2015. "All Writing Is Multimodal." In *Naming What We Know: Threshold Concepts of Writing Studies*, edited by Linda Adler-Kassner and Elizabeth Wardle, 42–43. Logan: Utah State University Press.

Barbara. 2010. "Literacy Narrative Final." Unpublished manuscript.

Bartholomae, David. 1985. "Inventing the University." In *When a Writer Can't Write: Studies in Writer's Block and Other Composing-Process Problems*, edited by Mike Rose, 134–65. New York: Guilford.

Bartholomae, David. 1995. "Writing with Teachers: A Conversation with Peter Elbow." *College Composition and Communication* 46 (1): 62–71. doi:10.2307/358870.

Bazerman, Charles. 2004. "Intertextualities: Volsinov, Bakhtin, Literacy Theory, and Literacy Studies." In *Bakhtinian Perspectives on Language, Literacy, and Learning*, edited by Arnetha F. Ball and Sarah Warshauer Freedman, 53–65. Cambridge: Cambridge University Press.

Berlin, James A. 1982. "Contemporary Composition: The Major Pedagogical Theories." *College English* 44 (8): 765–77.

Berkenkotter, Carol, Thomas N. Huckin, and John Ackerman. 1988. "Conventions, Conversations, and the Writer: Case Study of a Student in a Rhetoric Ph.D. Program." *Research in the Teaching of English* 22 (1): 9–44. http://www.jstor.org/stable/40171130.

Bishop, Wendy. 1990. *Something Old, Something New: College Writing Teachers and Classroom Change.* Carbondale: Southern Illinois University Press.

Bishop, Wendy. 1995. "The Literary Text and the Writing Classroom." *JAC* 15 (3): 435–54.

Bizzell, Patricia. 1982. "Cognition, Convention, and Certainty: What We Need to Know About Writing." *Pre/Text* 3 (3): 213–43.

Blake. 2010. "Literacy Narrative Draft." Unpublished manuscript.

Blake. 2010. "Literacy Narrative Final." Unpublished manuscript.

Blau, Sheridan. 2017. "How the Teaching of Literature in College Writing Classes Might Rescue Reading as It Never Has Before." In *Deep Reading: Teaching Reading in the Writing Classroom,* edited by Patrick Sullivan, Howard Tinberg, and Sheridan Blau, 265–90. Urbana, IL: NCTE.

Brandt, Deborah. 1998. "Sponsors of Literacy." *College Composition and Communication* 49 (2): 165–85. doi:10.2307/358929.

Brandt, Deborah. 2018. "Awakening to Literacy circa 1983." *College Composition and Communication* 69 (3): 503–10.

Brewer, Meaghan, and Kristen di Gennaro. 2018. "Naming What We Feel: Hierarchical Microaggressions and the Relationship between Composition and English Studies." *Composition Studies* 46 (2): 15–34.

Brodkey, Linda. 1996. *Writing Permitted in Designated Areas Only.* Minneapolis: University of Minnesota Press.

Bruffee, Kenneth. 1984. "Collaborative Learning and the 'Conversation of Mankind.'" *College English* 46 (7): 635–52. doi:10.2307/376924.

Buffington, Nancy, and Clyde Moneyhun. 1997. "A Conversation with Gerald Graff and Ira Shor." *JAC* 17 (1): 1–21.

Burke, Kenneth. 1966. *Language as Symbolic Action: Essays on Life, Literature, and Method.* Berkeley: University of California Press.

Burnham, Chris, and Rebecca Powell. 2013. "Expressive Pedagogy: Practice/Theory, Theory/Practice." In *A Guide to Composition Pedagogies,* 2nd ed., edited by Gary Tate, Amy Rupiper Taggart, Kurt Schick, and H. Brooke Hessler, 111–27. Oxford: Oxford University Press.

Butler, Octavia. 2003. *Kindred.* Boston: Beacon Press.

Canagarajah, Suresh. 2016. "Translingual Writing and Teacher Development in Composition." *College English* 78 (3): 265–73.

Carillo, Ellen. 2015. *Securing a Place for Reading in Composition: The Importance of Teaching for Transfer.* Logan: Utah State University Press.

Cole, Barbara, and Arabella Lyon. 2008. "Mentor or Magician: Reciprocities, Existing Ideologies, and Reflections of the Discipline." In *Stories of Mentoring: Theory and Praxis,* edited by Michelle F. Eble and Lynée Lewis Gaillet, 193–206. West Lafayette, IN: Parlor Press.

Coleman, David. 2011. "Bringing the Common Core to Life," April 28. http://usny.nysed.gov/rttt/docs/bringingthecommoncoretolife/fulltranscript.pdf.

Costino, Kimberly A., and Sunny Hyon. 2011. "Sidestepping Our 'Scare Words': Genre as a Possible Bridge between L1 and L2 Compositionists." *Journal of Second Language Writing* 20 (1): 24–44. doi: 10.1016/j.jslw.2010.12.001.

Crowley, Sharon. 1998. *Composition in the University: Historical and Polemical Essays.* Pittsburgh: University of Pittsburgh Press.

David. 2010. "Practicum Syllabus."

Dewey, John. 1944. *Democracy and Education: An Introduction to the Philosophy of Education.* New York: Free Press.

Dilks, Stephen, Regina Hansen, and Matthew Parfitt, eds. 2001. *Cultural Conversations: The Presence of the Past.* Boston: Bedford/St. Martin's.

Dobrin, Sidney, ed. 2005. *Don't Call It That: The Composition Practicum.* Urbana, IL: NCTE.

Dolmage, Jay. 2008. "Mapping Composition: Inviting Disability in the Front Door." In *Disability and the Teaching of Writing,* edited by Cynthia Lewiecki-Wilson and Brenda Jo Brueggemann, 14–27. Boston: Bedford/St. Martin's.

Downs, Doug. 2016. "What Is First-Year Composition?" In *A Rhetoric for Writing Program Administrators,* edited by Rita Malenczyk, 50–63. Andersen, SC: Parlor Press.

Downs, Doug, Jessie Moore, and Jeffrey Ringer. 2018. "Researching Transfer: Addressing the Challenges of Knowing What Works." Conference on College Composition and Communication. Respondents: Dana Driscoll, Elizabeth Wardle, and Kathleen Blake Yancey. Roundtable Leader: Irwin Weiser. Kansas City, MO, March 18.

Dryer, Dylan B. 2012. "At a Mirror, Darkly: The Imagined Undergraduate Writers of Ten Novice Composition Instructors." *College Composition and Communication* 63 (3): 420–52.

Duffelmeyer, Barb Blakely. 2005. "Not Just Showing Up to Class: New TAs, Critical Composition Pedagogy, and Multiliteracies" *WPA: Writing Program Administration* 28 (3): 31–56.

Durst, Russel. 1999. *Collision Course: Conflict, Negotiation, and Learning in College Composition.* Urbana, IL: NCTE.

Ebest, Sally Barr. 2005. *Changing the Way We Teach: Writing and Resistance in the Training of Teaching Assistants.* Carbondale: Southern Illinois University Press.

Ede, Lisa. 2004. *Situating Composition: Composition Studies and the Politics of Location.* Carbondale: Southern Illinois University Press.

Elbow, Peter. 1998. *Writing without Teachers.* New York: Oxford University Press.

Elbow, Peter. 2002. "The Cultures of Literature and Composition: What Could Each Learn from the Other?" *College English* 64 (5): 533–46. doi:10.2307/3250752.

Enos, Theresa. 2003. "Gender and Publishing Scholarship in Rhetoric and Composition." In *Feminism and Composition: A Critical Sourcebook,* edited by Gesa E. Kirsch, Faye Spencer Maor, Lance Massey, Lee Nickoson-Massey, and Mary P. Sheridan-Rabideau, 558–74. Boston: Bedford/St. Martin's.

Estrem, Heidi. 2015. "Disciplinary and Professional Identities Are Constructed through Writing." In *Naming What We Know: Threshold Concepts of Writing Studies,* edited by Linda Adler-Kassner and Elizabeth Wardle, 55–56. Logan: Utah State University Press.

Estrem, Heidi, and E. Shelley Reid. 2012. "What New Writing Teachers Talk about When They Talk about Teaching." *Pedagogy: Critical Approaches to Teaching Literacy, Language, Composition, and Culture* 12 (3): 449–80.

Farris, Christine. 1996. *Subject to Change: New Composition Instructors' Theory and Practice.* Cresskill, NJ: Hampton.

Fedukovich, Casie, and Megan Hall. 2016. "GTA Preparation as a Model for Cross-Tier Collaboration at North Carolina State University: A Program Profile." *Composition Forum* 33. http://compositionforum.com/issue/33/ncsu.php.

Finnegan, Ruth. 1973. "Literacy versus Non-literacy: The Great Divide?" In *Modes of Thought: Essays on Thinking in Western and Non-Western Societies,* edited by Robin Horton and Ruth Finnegan, 112–44. London: Faber & Faber.

"First-Year Writing Program Website." 2010. Public University.

Flower, Linda, and John R. Hayes. 1981. "A Cognitive Process Theory of Writing." *College Composition and Communication* 32 (4): 365–87. doi:10.2307/356600.

Flynn, Elizabeth. 2003. "Composing as a Woman." In *Feminism and Composition: A Critical Sourcebook,* edited by Gesa E. Kirsch, Faye Spencer Maor, Lance Massey, Lee Nickoson-Massey, and Mary P. Sheridan, 243–55. Boston: Bedford/St. Martin's.

Freire, Paulo. 2008. *Pedagogy of the Oppressed.* Translated by Myra Bergman Ramos. New York: Continuum.

Freire, Paulo, and Donaldo Macedo. 1987. *Literacy: Reading the Word and the World.* Westport, CT: Bergin & Garvey.

Freud, Sigmund. 2003. "The Uncanny." In *The Uncanny.* Translated by David McClintock, 121–62. London: Penguin.

Friedan, Betty. 2001. *The Feminine Mystique.* New York: Norton.

Garrett. 2010. "Literacy Narrative Draft." Unpublished manuscript.

Garrett. 2010. "Literacy Narrative Final." Unpublished manuscript.

Gearhart, Sally Miller. 1979. "The Womanization of Rhetoric." *Women's Studies International Quarterly* 2 (2): 195–201. doi: 10.1016/S0148-0685(79)91809-8.

Gee, James Paul. 1989. "Literacy, Discourse, and Linguistics." *Journal of Education* 171 (1): 5–17.

Gere, Anne Ruggles. 2009. *Initial Report on a Survey of CCCC Members.* Ann Arbor: Michigan State University, Squire Office of Policy Research.

Gere, Anne Ruggles, Jennifer Buehler, Christian Dallavis, and Victoria Shaw Haviland. 2009. "A Visibility Project: Learning to See How Preservice Teachers Take Up Culturally Responsive Pedagogy." *American Educational Research Journal* 46 (3): 816–52. doi: 10.3102/0002831209333182.

Gere, Anne Ruggles, Sarah C. Swofford, Naomi Silver, and Melody Pugh. 2015. "Interrogating Disciplines/Disciplinarity in WAC/WID: An Institutional Study." *College Composition and Communication* 67 (2): 243–66.

Glenn, Cheryl and Melissa A. Goldthwaite, eds. 2008. *The St. Martin's Guide to Teaching Writing,* 6th ed. Boston: Bedford/St. Martin's.

Goggin, Peter N. 2008. *Professing Literacy in Composition Studies.* Cresskill, NJ: Hampton.

Gold, David. 2012. "Remapping Revisionist Historiography." *College Composition and Communication* 64 (1): 15–34.

Goldblatt, Eli. 2007. *Because We Live Here: Sponsoring Literacy beyond the College Curriculum.* New York: Hampton.

Goldblatt, Eli. 2017. "Don't Call It Expressivism: Legacies of a 'Tacit Tradition.'" *College Composition and Communication* 68 (3): 438–65.

Goldsmith, Kevin. 2008. "Conceptual Poetics." Poetry Foundation. https://www.poetryfoundation.org/harriet/2008/06/conceptual-poetics-kenneth-goldsmith.

Good, Tina Lavonne, and Leanne B. Warshauer, eds. 2000. *In Our Own Voice: Graduate Students Teach Writing.* Boston: Allyn and Bacon.

Graff, Harvey. 2001. "The Nineteenth-Century Origins of Our Times." *Literacy: A Critical Sourcebook,* edited by Ellen Cushman, Eugene R. Kintgen, Barry M. Kroll, and Mike Rose, 211–33. Boston: Bedford/St. Martin's.

Graff, Harvey J., and John Duffy. 2008. "Literacy Myths." In *Encyclopedia of Language and Education.* Vol. 2, *Literacy,* 2nd ed., edited by Brian V. Street and Nancy H. Hornberger, 41–52. New York: Springer Science and Business.

Gramer, Rachel. 2017. *Stories at Work: Restorying Narratives of New Teachers' Identity Learning in Writing Studies.* PhD Diss., University of Louisville. Electronic Theses and Dissertations (Paper 2678). doi: 10.18297/etd/2678.

Grouling, Jennifer. 2015. "Resistance and Identity Formation: The Journey of the Graduate Student-Teacher." *Composition Forum* 32. http://compositionforum.com/issue/32/resistance.php.

Grutsch McKinney, Jackie, and Elizabeth Chiseri-Strater. 2003. "Inventing the Teacherly Self: Positioning Journals in the TA Seminar." *WPA: Writing Program Administration* 27 (1–2): 59–74.

Guerra, Juan C., and Anis Bawarshi. 2005. "Managing Transitions: Reorienting Perceptions in a Practicum Course." In *Don't Call It That: The Composition Practicum,* edited by Sidney Dobrin, 43–66. Urbana, IL: NCTE.

Hansen, Kristine. 2018. "Discipline and Profession: Can the Field of Rhetoric and Writing Be Both?" In *Composition, Rhetoric, and Disciplinarity,* edited by Rita Malenczyk, Susan Miller-Cochran, Elizabeth Wardle, and Kathleen Blake Yancey, 134–58. Logan: Utah State University Press.

Harker, Michael. 2015. *The Lure of Literacy: A Critical Reception of the Compulsory Composition Debate.* Albany: SUNY Press.

Harris, Joseph. 1997. *A Teaching Subject: Composition Since 1966.* Upper Saddle River, NJ: Prentice.

Heath, Shirley Brice, and Brian V. Street. 2008. *On Ethnography: Approaches to Language and Literacy Research.* New York: Teachers College Press.

Hesse, Douglas. 1993. "Teachers as Students, Reflecting Resistance." *College Composition and Communication* 44 (2): 224–31. doi:10.2307/358840.

Hesse, Douglas. 2010. "The Place of Creative Writing in Composition Studies." *College Composition and Communication* 62 (1): 31–52.

Hillocks, George. 1995. *Teaching Writing as a Reflective Practice.* New York: Teacher's College Press.

Hirsch, E. D. 1988. *Cultural Literacy: What Every American Needs to Know.* New York: Vintage.

Howard, Rebecca Moore. 2014. "Why This Humanist Codes." *Research in the Teaching of English* 49 (1): 75–81.

Jago, Carol. 2009. *Crash! The Currency Crisis in American Culture*. http://www.ncte .org/library/NCTEFiles/Press/Jago_final.pdf.

Jarratt, Susan C. 2003. "Feminism and Composition: The Case for Conflict." *Feminism and Composition: A Critical Sourcebook*, edited by Gesa E. Kirsch, Faye Spencer Maor, Lance Massey, Lee Nickoson-Massey, and Mary P. Sheridan, 263–80. Boston: Bedford/St. Martin's.

Jolliffe, David A., and Allison Harl. 2008. "Studying the 'Reading Transition' from High School to College: What Are Our Students Reading and Why?" *College English* 70 (6): 599–617.

Jordi. 2010. "Literacy Narrative Draft." Unpublished manuscript.

Jordi. 2010. "Literacy Narrative Final." Unpublished manuscript.

Karen. 2010. "Literacy Narrative Draft." Unpublished manuscript.

Karen. 2010. "Literacy Narrative Final." Unpublished manuscript.

Knoblauch, C. H. 1990. "Literacy and the Politics of Education." In *The Right to Literacy*, edited by Andrea Lunsford, Helene Moglen, and James Slevin, 74–80. New York: Modern Language Association.

Kristeva, Julia. 1980. *Desire in Language: A Semiotic Approach to Literature and Art*. New York: Columbia University Press.

Kynard, Carmen. 2015. "Teaching While Black: Witnessing and Countering Disciplinary Whiteness, Racial Violence, and University Race-Management." *Literacy in Composition Studies* 3 (1): 1–20. http://licsjournal.org/OJS/index .php/LiCS/article/view/62/84.

Leon, Kendall, Laurie A. Pinkert, and Kathryn Trauth Taylor. 2017. "Developing Accounts of Instructor Learning: Recognizing the Impacts of Service-Learning Pedagogies on Writing Teachers." *Composition Studies* 45 (1): 39–58.

Lily. 2010. "Literacy Narrative Draft." Unpublished manuscript.

Lily. 2010. "Literacy Narrative Final." Unpublished manuscript.

Lindemann, Erika. 1993. "Freshman Composition: No Place for Literature." *College English* 55 (3): 311–16. doi:10.2307/378743.

Maher, Jennifer Helene. 2018. "Embracing the Virtue in Our Disciplinarity." In *Composition, Rhetoric, and Disciplinarity*, edited by Rita Malenczyk, Susan Miller-Cochran, Elizabeth Wardle, and Kathleen Blake Yancey, 161–84. Logan: Utah State University Press.

Malenczyk, Rita, Susan Miller-Cochran, Elizabeth Wardle, and Kathleen Blake Yancey, eds. 2018. *Composition, Rhetoric, and Disciplinarity*. Logan: Utah State University Press.

Meyer, Jan, and Ray Land, eds. 2006. *Overcoming Barriers to Student Understanding: Threshold Concepts and Troublesome Knowledge*. New York: Routledge.

Miller, Richard E. 1998. "The Arts of Complicity: Pragmatism and the Culture of Schooling." *College English* 61(1): 10–28. doi:10.2307/379055.

Miller, Susan. 1991. *Textual Carnivals: The Politics of Composition*. Carbondale: Southern Illinois University Press.

Miller, Thomas P. 2011. *The Evolution of College English: Literacy Studies from the Puritans to the Postmoderns*. Pittsburgh: University of Pittsburgh Press.

Miller, Susan Kay, Rochelle Rodrigo, Veronica Pantoja, and Duane Roen. 2005. "The Composition Practicum as Professional Development." In *Don't Call It That: The Composition Practicum*, edited by Sidney Dobrin, 82–97. Urbana, IL: NCTE.

Moll, Luis, Cathy Amanti, Deborah Neff, and Norma Gonzalez. 1992. "Funds of Knowledge for Teaching: Using a Qualitative Approach to Connect Homes and Classrooms." *Theory into Practice* 31 (2): 132–41.

Obermark, Lauren, Elizabeth Brewer, and Kay Halasek. 2015. "Moving from the One and Done to a Culture of Collaboration: Revising Professional Development for TAs." *WPA: Writing Program Administration* 39 (1): 32–53.

Perkins, David. 2006. "Constructivism and Troublesome Knowledge." In *Overcoming Barriers to Student Understanding: Threshold Concepts and Troublesome Knowledge*, edited by Jan Meyer and Ray Land, 33–47. New York: Routledge.

Perkins, David, and Gavriel Salomon. 1988. "Teaching for Transfer." *Educational Leadership* 46 (1): 22–32.

Porter, James E. 1986. "Intertextuality and the Discourse Community." *Rhetoric Review* 5 (1): 34–47. https://www.jstor.org/stable/466015.

Qualley, Donna. 2016. "Building a Conceptual Topography of the Transfer Terrain." In *Critical Transitions: Writing and the Question of Transfer*, edited by Chris M. Anson and Jessie Moore, 69–106. Boulder: University Press of Colorado.

Rankin, Elizabeth. 1994. *Seeing Yourself as a Teacher: Conversations with Five New Teachers in a University Writing Program*. Urbana, IL: NCTE.

Reid, E. Shelley. 2007. "Anxieties of Influencers: Composition Pedagogy in the 21st Century." *WPA: Writing Program Administration* 31 (1/2): 241–49.

Reid, E. Shelley. 2009. "Teaching Writing Teachers Writing: Difficulty, Exploration, and Critical Reflection." *College Composition and Communication* 61 (2): 197–221.

Reid, E. Shelley, Heidi Estrem, and Marcia Belcheir. 2012. "The Effects of Writing Pedagogy Education on Graduate Teaching Assistants' Approaches to Teaching Composition." *WPA: Writing Program Administration* 36 (1): 32–73.

Reiff, Mary Jo, and Anis Bawarshi. 2011. "Tracing Discursive Resources: How Students Use Prior Genre Knowledge to Negotiate New Writing Contexts in First-Year Composition." *Written Communication* 28 (3): 312–37.

Restaino, Jessica. 2012. *First Semester: Graduate Students, Teaching Writing, and the Challenge of Middle Ground*. Carbondale: Southern Illinois University Press.

Ritter, Kelly. 2012. "'Ladies Who Don't Know Us Correct Our Papers': Postwar Lay Reader Programs and Twenty-First Century Contingent Labor in First-Year Writing." *College Composition and Communication* 63 (3): 387–419.

Roeder, Tara, and Roseanne Gatto, eds. 2015. *Critical Expressivism: Theory and Practice in the Composition Classroom*. Anderson, SC: Parlor Press.

Roozen, Kevin. 2015a. "Texts Get Their Meaning from Other Texts." In *Naming What We Know; Threshold Concepts of Writing Studies*, edited by Linda Adler-Kassner and Elizabeth Wardle, 44–47. Logan: Utah State University Press.

Roozen, Kevin. 2015b. "Writing Is a Social and Rhetorical Activity." In *Naming What We Know: Threshold Concepts of Writing Studies*, edited by Adler-Kassner and Wardle, 17–18. Logan: Utah State University Press.

Royster, Jacqueline Jones. 1996. "When the First Voice You Hear Is Not Your Own." *College Composition and Communication* 47 (1): 29–40. doi:10.2307/358272.

Rupiper Taggart, Amy, and Margaret Lowry. 2011. "Cohorts, Grading, and Ethos: Listening to TAs Enhances Teacher Preparation." *WPA: Writing Program Administration* 34 (2): 89–114.

Ryan, Kathleen J., and Tarez Samra Graban. 2009. "Theorizing Feminist Pragmatic Rhetoric as a Communicative Art for the Composition Practicum." *College Composition and Communication* 61 (1): W277–W299.

Schell, Eileen E. 1998. *Gypsy Academics and Mother-Teachers: Gender, Contingent Labor, and Writing Instruction.* Portsmouth, NH: Boynton/Cook.

Schiavone, Aubrey, and Anna V. Knutson. 2017. "Pedagogy at the Crossroads: Instructor Identity, Social Class Consciousness, and Reflective Teaching Practice." In *Class in the Composition Classroom,* edited by Genesea M. Carter and William H. Thelin. Logan: Utah State University Press.

Schieber, Danica L. 2016. "Invisible Transfer: An Unexpected Finding in the Pursuit of Transfer." *Business and Professional Communication Quarterly* 79 (4): 464–86. doi:10.1177/2329490616660816.

Scribner, Sylvia. 1984. "Literacy in Three Metaphors." *American Journal of Education* 93 (1): 6–21. doi:10.1086/443783.

Shipka, Jody. 2013. "Including, but Not Limited to, the Digital." In *Multimodal Literacies and Emerging Genres,* edited by Tracey Bowen and Carl Whithaus, 73–89. Pittsburgh: University of Pittsburgh Press.

Smit, David W. 2004. *The End of Composition Studies.* Carbondale: Southern Illinois University Press.

Smith, Michael W., and Dorothy S. Strickland. 2001. "Complements or Conflicts: Conceptions of Discussion and Multicultural Literature in a Teacher-as-Readers Discussion Group." *Journal of Literacy Research* 33 (1): 137–67. doi:10.1080/10862960109548105.

Stancliff, Michael, and Maureen Daly Goggin. 2007. "What's Theorizing Got to Do with It? Teaching Theory as Resourceful Conflict and Reflection in TA Preparation." *WPA: Writing Program Administration* 30 (3): 11–28.

Stuckey, Elspeth. 1991. *The Violence of Literacy.* Portsmouth, NH: Heinemann.

Taczak, Kara, and Kathleen Blake Yancey. 2015. "Threshold Concepts in Rhetoric and Composition Doctoral Education: The Delivered, Lived, and Experienced Curriculum." In *Naming What We Know: Threshold Concepts of Writing Studies,* edited by Linda Adler-Kassner and Elizabeth Wardle, 140–54. Logan: Utah State University Press.

Tate, Gary, Amy Rupiper-Taggart, Kurt Schick, and H. Brooke Hessler, eds. 2013. *A Guide to Composition Pedagogies.* 2nd ed. Oxford: Oxford University Press.

Taylor, Marcy, and Jennifer L. Holberg. 1999. "Tales of Neglect and Sadism: Disciplinarity and the Figuring of the Graduate Student in Composition." *College Composition and Communication* 50 (4): 607–25. doi:10.2307/358483.

Vidali, Amy. 2008. "Discourses of Disability and Basic Writing." In *Disability and the Teaching of Writing,* edited by Cynthia Lewiecki-Wilson and Brenda Jo Brueggemann, 40–55. Boston: Bedford/St. Martin's.

Villanueva, Victor. 2015. "Writing Provides a Representation of Ideologies and Identities." In *Naming What We Know: Threshold Concepts of Writing Studies,* edited by Linda Adler-Kassner and Elizabeth Wardle, 57–58. Logan: Utah State University Press.

Waite, Stacey. 2016. "The Unavailable Means of Persuasion: A Queer Ethos for Feminist Writers and Teachers." In *Rethinking Ethos: A Feminist Ecological Approach to Rhetoric,* edited by Kathleen J. Ryan, Nancy Myers, and Rebecca Jones, 71–88. Carbondale: Southern Illinois University Press.

Wardle, Elizabeth. 2014. "Considering What It Means to Teach 'Composition' in the Twenty-First Century." *College Composition and Communication* 65 (4): 659–71.

Warner, John. 2018. "Recommended Reading for the Start of the Semester." *Inside Higher Ed*, June 9. https://www.insidehighered.com/blogs/just-visiting/recommended-reading-start-semester.

Welch, Nancy. 1993. "Resisting the Faith: Conversion, Resistance, and the Training of Teachers." *College English*, 55 (4): 387–401. doi:10.2307/378649.

Wilhoit, Stephen. 2002. "Recent Trends in TA Instruction: A Bibliographic Essay." *Preparing College Teachers of Writing: Histories, Theories, Programs, Practices*, edited by Betty P. Pytlik and Sarah Liggett. Oxford: Oxford University Press.

Yancey, Kathleen Blake. 2015. "Coming to Terms: Composition/Rhetoric, Threshold Concepts, and a Disciplinary Core." In *Naming What We Know: Threshold Concepts of Writing Studies*, edited by Linda Adler-Kassner and Elizabeth Wardle, xvii–xxxi. Logan: Utah State University Press.

Yancey, Kathleen Blake. 2018. "Mapping the Turn to Disciplinarity: A Historical Analysis of Composition's Trajectory and Its Current Movement." In *Composition, Rhetoric, and Disciplinarity*, edited by Rita Malenczyk, Susan Miller-Cochran, Elizabeth Wardle, and Kathleen Blake Yancey, 15–35. Logan: Utah State University Press.

Yancey, Kathleen Blake, Liane Robertson, and Kara Taczak. 2014. *Writing across Contexts: Transfer, Composition, and Sites of Writing*. Logan: Utah State University Press.

ABOUT THE AUTHOR

Meaghan Brewer is an assistant professor at Pace University, where she directs the writing across the curriculum program and teaches courses in composition, rhetoric, and literacy. Her research includes teacher education for graduate students, literacy, disciplinarity, and women's science education. She has published articles in *Peitho*, *Composition Studies*, *Composition Forum*, *Applied Linguistics Review*, and the *Journal of Adolescent and Adult Literacy*.

INDEX

narratives. *See* literacy narratives
New Criticism, 90, 92
noncompliance, 25
nonviolence, as theme, 112–13
nurturing, 46

online writing community, 103
oppression, 125
Other, 125

paintings, as multimodal text, 112
Paley, Karen, 123
pedagogical strategies, 23
pedagogy, 6–7, 39, 116, 129
peers, as resources/mentors, 132, 133
Pelligrino, James W., 124
people of color: and oppressive discourse, 50; voices, 39
Perkins, David, 101, 126
personal growth, literacy for, 6, 20, 30, 31, 33–34, 35, 36, 40–41, 45–51
personal narrative, 38
personal voice, writer's, 34–35
phonics, 44
plagiarism, 95
poetry, 55
power relationships, 99
practice, and theory, 140
practicum, 6, 8, 9, 12, 32, 155, 167(n3); identity and resistance in, 24–27; influence of, 88, 133–34, 138–39; literacy concepts, 139–49; literacy narratives, 10–11; methodology of, 13–14; schedule, 165–66
prior knowledge, role of, 28–29
process movement, 33
Protestants, home schooling, 77–78
Public University, 7–8, 9, 10
Pugh, Melody, 121

Qualley, Donna, 126
queer, voices, 39
queer theory, queerness, 94

race, 113–14, 115, 116, 146, 167(n5)
Rankin, Elizabeth, on resistance, 24
reading, 30, 91, 146–47; in classroom practice, 79–81; conscientious,

78–79; cultural literacy approach to, 72–73, 80–89; textual hierarchies, 73–74
rebellion, 25
reflexive instrumentalism, 18
Reid, E. Shelley, 4, 129, 151; on resistance, 24, 25; on teaching experience, 135–36
Reiff, Mary Jo, 29, 108
religious background, and cultural literacy, 77–79
remix model, 28
representation, 115; writing as, 113–17
research assistants, 129
resistance, 12, 121; graduate instructor, 11, 60–61; as productive, 24–25; students, 148–49
Restaino, Jessica, 5, 128
retrospection, of experiences, 126–27
rhetoric, 17, 103–4, 108
rhetoric and composition. *See* composition and rhetoric
Rhetoric, Composition, and Disciplinarity (Malenczyk et al.), 150
Rhodes, Jacqueline, 94
ritual: literacy as, 69, 72–76; reading as, 78
Robertson, Liane, 29, 108; on transfer practices, 27–28
romantic ideology, 41
Roosevelt, Theodore, 80
Roozen, Kevin, 120; on intertextuality, 109–10
Rosenblatt, Louise, 133
Royster, Jacqueline Jones, 39, 105
rule breakers, 45
Rupiper, Amy, 100

St. Martin's Guide to Teaching Writing, The (Berthoff), 133–34, 138
Saloman, Gavriel, 126
Salvatori, Mariolina, 72
Scary Stories to Tell in the Dark (Schwartz), 73
Schick, Kurt, 100
Schieber, Danica, 29
school, as agent of oppression, 42, 44–45